MARGARET BONDS

In her lifetime, African American composer Margaret Bonds was classical music's most intrepid social-justice activist. Her *Montgomery Variations* (1964) and setting of W. E. B. Du Bois's iconic Civil Rights *Credo* (1965–7) were the musical summits of her activism. These works fell into obscurity after Bonds's death but were recovered and published in 2020. Since widely performed, they are finally gaining a recognition long denied. This incisive book situates *The Montgomery Variations* and *Credo* in their political and biographical contexts, providing an interdisciplinary exploration that brings notables including Harry Burleigh, W. E. B. and Shirley Graham Du Bois, Martin Luther King, Jr., Abbie Mitchell, Ned Rorem, and – especially – Langston Hughes into the works' collective ambit. The resulting brief, but instructive, appraisal introduces readers to two masterworks whose recovery is a modern musical milestone – and reveals their message to be one that, though born in the mid-twentieth century, speaks directly to our own time.

JOHN MICHAEL COOPER is Professor of Music at Southwestern University. He is the author of the first book-length biography of Margaret Bonds (forthcoming), the *Historical Dictionary of Romantic Music* (2nd ed., 2023), and three books on Felix Mendelssohn, as well as editor of numerous compositions by Bonds and Florence Price.

T0334708

NEW CAMBRIDGE MUSIC HANDBOOKS

Series Editor

NICOLE GRIMES, UNIVERSITY OF CALIFORNIA–IRVINE

The New Cambridge Music Handbooks series provides accessible introductions to landmarks in music history, written by leading experts in their field. Encompassing a wide range of musical styles and genres, it embraces the music of hitherto under-represented creators as well as re-imagining works from the established canon. It will enrich the musical experience of students, scholars, listeners and performers alike.

Books in the Series

Hensel: String Quartet in E flat
Benedict Taylor

Berlioz: Symphonie Fantastique
Julian Rushton

Margaret Bonds: The Montgomery Variations *and Du Bois* Credo
John Michael Cooper

Schoenberg: 'Night Music', Verklärte Nacht and Erwartung
Arnold Whittall

Forthcoming Titles

Schubert: The 'Great' Symphony in C major
Suzannah Clark

Bach: The Cello Suites
Edward Klorman

Clara Schumann: Piano Concerto in A minor Op. 7
Julie Pedneault-Deslauriers

Donizetti: Lucia di Lammermoor
Mark Pottinger

Beethoven: String Quartet Op. 130
Elaine Sisman

Louise Farrenc: Nonet for Winds and Strings
Marie Sumner Lott

Cavalleria rusticana *and* Pagliacci
Alexandra Wilson

MARGARET BONDS

The *Montgomery Variations* and Du Bois *Credo*

JOHN MICHAEL COOPER
Southwestern University

CAMBRIDGE
UNIVERSITY PRESS

CAMBRIDGE
UNIVERSITY PRESS

Shaftesbury Road, Cambridge CB2 8EA, United Kingdom

One Liberty Plaza, 20th Floor, New York, NY 10006, USA

477 Williamstown Road, Port Melbourne, VIC 3207, Australia

314–321, 3rd Floor, Plot 3, Splendor Forum, Jasola District Centre, New Delhi – 110025, India

103 Penang Road, #05–06/07, Visioncrest Commercial, Singapore 238467

Cambridge University Press is part of Cambridge University Press & Assessment, a department of the University of Cambridge.

We share the University's mission to contribute to society through the pursuit of education, learning and research at the highest international levels of excellence.

www.cambridge.org
Information on this title: www.cambridge.org/9781316511763

DOI: 10.1017/9781009053792

First published 2024

A catalogue record for this publication is available from the British Library.

Library of Congress Cataloging-in-Publication Data
NAMES: Cooper, John Michael, author.
TITLE: Margaret Bonds : the Montgomery variations and Du Bois 'Credo' / John Michael Cooper.
DESCRIPTION: [1.] | Cambridge, United Kingdom ; New York : Cambridge University Press, 2023. | Series: MUHB new Cambridge music handbooks | Includes bibliographical references and index.
IDENTIFIERS: LCCN 2023025808 (print) | LCCN 2023025809 (ebook) | ISBN 9781316511763 (hardcover) | ISBN 9781009054577 (paperback) | ISBN 9781009053792 (ebook)
SUBJECTS: LCSH: Bonds, Margaret – Criticism and interpretation. | Bonds, Margaret. Montgomery variations. | Bonds, Margaret. Credo. | Civil rights movements – United States. | Music and race – United States – History – 20th century | Music – United States – 20th century – History and criticism.
CLASSIFICATION: LCC ML410.B69806 C65 2023 (print) | LCC ML410.B69806 (ebook) | DDC 780.92–dc23/eng/20230601
LC record available at https://lccn.loc.gov/2023025808
LC ebook record available at https://lccn.loc.gov/2023025809

ISBN 978-1-316-51176-3 Hardback
ISBN 978-1-009-05457-7 Paperback

CONTENTS

FIGURES

MUSIC EXAMPLES

PREFACE

On the face of it this book is about one composer and two pieces of music. That much is true, but it is only the surface. For just behind that composer, Margaret Bonds (1913–72), stands W. E. B. Du Bois (1868–1963), one of the modern era's boldest and most brilliant scholars of race relations and advocates for racial justice and social justice generally. Alongside the two of them are Abbie Mitchell (1864–1960), the pioneering German-Jewish/African American actress and soprano who performed the role of Clara in the premiere of Gershwin's *Porgy and Bess*; Langston Hughes (1902–67), Bonds's closest friend and career-long collaborator; and Martin Luther King, Jr. (1929–68), whose poetic eloquence and visionary commitment to nonviolent racial justice inspired the whole world in the late 1950s and 1960s, and continues to do so. Their voices extend from the 1880s into the 1970s and still resonate powerfully today, and the geographic terrain through which those voices resound in these works envoices peoples in not only the United States, but also Europe, Africa, and (especially for Bonds) Asia. Finally, this formidable cast of characters holds aloft, in music and word, act and idea, the banner of the quest for racial justice, gender justice, and global equality, a banner that few readers of this book will regard as inimical.

That is a great deal of chronological, conceptual, ideological, and of course musical ground to cover in this short handbook, but it is fertile soil. This might seem self-evident, given the social intensity and political energy of the US Civil Rights Movement that occasioned the two works that are featured here, but it owes also to the power of Du Bois's thinking and writing, the richness of Bonds's hitherto largely unexplored correspondence, and not least the brilliance and depth of her music itself. Bonds was a passionate social-justice advocate and a prolific correspondent, and her musical imagination was commensurately voluble. This short book serves as an invitation to delve deeper and learn more about the prodigious mind and imagination and the even more remarkable music of the extraordinary Margaret Bonds.

Rediscovering or Recovering?

Latter-day commentators sometimes portray a recent resurgence of interest in composers of the African diaspora (most notably Margaret Bonds and Florence Price) as a "rediscovery,"[1] but a more nuanced approach helps to understand how two so obviously important works as *The Montgomery Variations* and the *Credo* have remained largely unheard for more than half a century despite their obvious topicality in the musical discourses of the 1960s, their importance in Bonds's output, and their timeliness today. Although many constituencies of classical music are predisposed to view previously obscure mid-twentieth-century African American composers and their music as relatively recent Black incursions into patently White spaces, and thus as "rediscovered," this perspective and its resultant Othering of African diasporic composers (including Margaret Bonds) are artifices of the systemic racism of White concert music's culture and historiography, especially in the United States: a society more discomfited by the acronym *BLM* than by the acronym *KKK* will naturally regard Black lives and Black voices as outsiders to the hallowed halls of Western classical music. In fact, these composers' names were never forgotten in Black communities, and some of their music has never been forgotten, either.[2] To speak of a "rediscovery" of Margaret Bonds or any other Black composer is thus inappropriate, for such an assertion perpetuates the White gaze that marginalized those composers to begin with.

There is, though, a Margaret Bonds to be *recovered*.[3] Although the canon-obsessed establishment of classical music marginalized her during the half-century following her death, that neglect never quite reached the point of erasure. During that same half-century, Black scholars and allies continued to explore Bonds's genius in their writings, Black performers and allies kept her music alive by including the handful of familiar pieces in recitals and recordings, audiences and critics continued to respond enthusiastically, and archivists and librarians assiduously preserved the priceless music manuscripts, letters, press clippings, postcards, photographs, and tape-recorded interviews that document her rich legacy.[4] The two works that are the centerpiece of this book are a case in point. After the death in 2011 of Bonds's daughter, Djane Richardson (b. 1946), a sizable trove of Bonds documents went to a book fair in Washington, DC, failed to sell, and was left beside a dumpster when the fair closed. Found by a collector, it ended up in the Booth Family Center for Special Collections at Georgetown University (Washington, DC).[5] And this very collection is the one that contains the sole surviving autographs for *The Montgomery Variations* and the orchestral version of the *Credo*, as well as a copy of the piano-vocal score of the latter containing autograph annotations from the composer. With their autographs having been literally rescued from the landfill by a collector and a university library, both works are now published.[6]

Music history's other posthumous recoveries offer room for optimism where the recovery of Margaret Bonds's legacy is concerned, for the processes of recovering that legacy resemble those by which early nineteenth-century Europeans (German and other) recovered the legacy of J. S. Bach – whose influence on *The Montgomery Variations* and the *Credo* is, as we shall see, significant, and whom Bonds herself referred to as "the father of all in Music."[7] Although the 1829 Berlin performances of the *St. Matthew Passion* are sometimes portrayed as a "rediscovery" that catapulted Bach into the public limelight and launched the Bach revival, the cultural memory of that composer and his legacy were in fact carefully stewarded over the preceding decades by his pupils, his sons, and a close-knit network of performers and institutions.[8] Agricola, Kirnberger, Kollmann, and C. P. E. Bach (among others) cultivated a continuing presence for Bach's teachings and style in their treatises. Fanny von Arnstein and Sarah Itzig Levy kept his music alive in their influential salons. Rochlitz and Forkel formulated biographical accounts that cast Bach as a saintly summit of a golden age of German music, while publishers such as Simrock (Bonn) and Breitkopf & Härtel (Leipzig) published selections of his music. And performers and institutions such as Muzio Clementi, Samuel Wesley, C. F. Horn, and of course the Berlin

Singakademie under the directorship of Fasch and Zelter ensured that the sounds of his music never passed into complete silence.

This conservationist work aptly parallels the means by which Margaret Bonds's name and memory have been sustained in the past half-century. And so, just as Felix Mendelssohn Bartholdy's 1829 performances of the *St. Matthew Passion* and Fanny Mendelssohn Hensel's Bach performances in her *Sonntagsmusiken* were not rediscoveries at all, but rather stations in a decades-long process of recovery, we may hope that Margaret Bonds will also be able to reenter the public musical discourse with the dynamic force and brilliance for which she was known in her own time. The stakes could hardly be higher – for the cast of characters listed at the beginning of these remarks, like the two works that form the center-piece of this book and Margaret Bonds herself, gave proud and unswerving voice to the quest for racial justice, gender justice, and global equality.

***

To ascribe a societal mission of the sort that motivated Bonds to Sebastian Bach would be, at best, a stretch. Nevertheless, even setting aside Bonds's reverence for Bach and his influence (along with that of Richard Strauss) on the two works that are the subject of this book, Bach and Bonds both had to negotiate musically disparate stylistic spheres in constructing their own respective public identities. In Bach's music this negotiation plays out pri-marily through his essays in German, French, and Italian styles and his frequent contrapositions of *stile antico* versus *stile mo-derno*. Stylistic negotiations of these contrasting musical spheres are integral or even essential to his art, and central to the vener-ation unanimously afforded today's recovered and more authentic Bach. Similarly, the stylistic eclecticism of Margaret Bonds's music is a defining feature of her identity and part of the immedi-acy of her musical language – and, indeed, her deft reconciliations of the incongruities between popular and classical, Black and White, spiritual and jazz and blues, deeply rooted in her experi-ences in Black churches, where in most denominations (including A. M. E., Baptist, Methodist, and Roman Catholic) those genres freely commingled, are rarely if ever surpassed in their brilliance, anywhere in any repertoire. For example, *The Ballad of the Brown King*, while outwardly a classical cantata, is suffused with call-and-response textures, calypso rhythms, gospel, and jazz; Bonds later recalled that "it's really jazz,"[9] and while composing it she surprised even herself with the depth of this stylistic synthesis, writing to Langston Hughes: "Tonight after I finished writing 'Sing of the King Who Was Tall and Brown' [No. VII of the revised version] I realized it can be done by the Modern Jazz Quartet without any words."[10]

But there is an important difference: Bach's negotiations of stylistic alterities were strictly voluntary, and Bonds's, while at least partly intentional, were inevitably bound up with the relentless segregational musical practices of the institutions of concert music and the world that she, as a woman of color, occupied to her dying day. That world prescribed certain genres and styles – chiefly blues, dances, gospel, jazz, and spirituals – for Black composers and "small forms" for women composers; but for Blacks and women to cross the color line and gender line, writing in classical idioms and/or larger forms, was for them, in the eyes of Whites, to transgress. Such transgressions, inevitably, were dismissed or ignored altogether, and what headway they made in breaking through the invisible but potent barriers that kept composers of color and women on the peripheries of the institutions of male-dominated White classical music was generally doomed to historiographic erasure – the sort of virtual erasure that has been the fate of most of Margaret Bonds's music (including *The Montgomery Variations* and *Credo*).

Margaret Bonds's refusal to be kept out of the White-dominated concert hall was a by-product of her Black feminism – an outlook that she shared with influential music critic Nora Holt (1885–1974). As is well known, Black feminism is not an outgrowth of non-Black feminism or any other movement but was born of the unique fusion of racism, classism, and sexism that Black women constantly face. It acknowledges that Black women's needs and perspectives differ profoundly from those of White women and Black men, and it argues that these forces of oppression, because of their inseparability, must be fought simultaneously.

It is an outlook, in other words, decidedly resistant to deferential obeisance to racially delineated patriarchal spaces. Despite personal disagreements,[11] Bonds clearly respected Holt's navigation of these treacherous spaces and may have followed her lead. Holt, in addition to her work as a soprano, pianist, composer, and music critic, was cofounder of the National Association of Negro Musicians, an organization in which Bonds, too, exerted leadership throughout her professional career. More substantively, Holt's two-pronged strategy for breaking through the barriers that kept Blacks out of White classical institutions may also be applied to Bonds.[12] One prong of this strategy was pedagogy and what Lucy Caplan has termed Holt's "communal approach to knowledge production"[13] among African Americans – Holt through her criticism and her long-running radio show, Bonds through her teaching and her frequent lectures. The other prong – a recognition of the "generative possibilities of racial difference"[14] – is more complex. Acknowledging the virtually inevitable inauthenticity of White representations of Black identity in music, it affirmed that Black artists' attempts to "whitewash" their music in order to assimilate into dominant White idioms was inherently false and doomed to aesthetic failure because of their denial of the feature that was actually their music's greatest aesthetic strength: its Blackness.

The first of these issues and the problems it produced is encountered in Bonds's correspondence as early as 1937, in her response to what she called "a lousy Negro play written by a white man."[15] The second is reflected in the overtness of Bonds's cultivation of Black idioms within genres and styles that are stereotypically White: the use of calypso, gospel, and jazz in a classical cantata in *The Ballad of the Brown King* and of an African American spiritual as the cantus firmus in a Bachian chorale cantata in *Simon Bore the Cross* (see Chapter 1); employing a spiritual and Black experience as theme and subject of a large and cyclical orchestral variation set in *The Montgomery Variations* (see Chapter 2); the importance of the genre of gospel song to the *Credo* (see Chapter 3). These transgressive border-crossings, each rich and complex in its own way, are arguably the most valuable tools modern scholars and other musicians have at our disposal as we seek to recover the nearly erased legacy of Margaret Bonds on her own, authentic terms rather than in some romanticized or otherwise anachronistic fashion. Although the ramifications of these issues cannot be fully explored here, suffice it to note that they are (among other things) sociological and historiographic, not just compositional and stylistic. Because of the profoundly segregated structures of life, including musical life, in the US (the political and racial arena that was home to the text, events, and music of *The Montgomery Variations* and *Credo*), the use of music or musical styles associated with one side of the color line in the context of the other was inherently transgressive as a political gesture. For example, the use of a spiritual was never *just* the use of a spiritual, nor was it *just* a religious gesture or even *just* a communal religious one. Rather, because spirituals (dubbed "the sorrow songs" by W. E. B. Du Bois[16]) were emblematic of Black Americans' ancestral heritage, of the importance of the Black church in the lives of many African Americans, and of the lived experiences and lived sufferings of Black folk generally, for Margaret Bonds to use the spiritual "I Want Jesus to Walk with Me" as the basis of *The Montgomery Variations* was not only germane to that work's program, but also transgressive. By inserting into the institutions of concert music a Black presence that was by convention and (in the South) by law segregated out from those institutions, it represented a lance thrown down before White domination in those institutions. The same is true of her allusions to gospel songs, jazz, and spirituals. As an African American and a woman, Bonds lived with the realities of systemic racism and systemic sexism every day of her life, and her correspondence and biography demonstrate that she chafed at them, fought them at every turn. That resistance was amply modeled for her in the Black churches in which she was raised, and where she worked as choir director for much of her career, for as Portia K. Maultsby and others have shown, Black churches of various denominations – A. M. E., Baptist, Methodist, Roman Catholic – cultivated both stereotypically "White" (i.e., Euro-American classical) and Black repertoires.[17] The meaningfulness of her pointed insertions of (as it were) an unwelcome dark-skinned female guest into the sacralized domain of the musical canon, dominated as it was by White males, should not be underestimated.

Nor should we forget that Bonds, ever a voracious consumer of music and one whose education at Northwestern University included at least four music history survey courses, would have been aware of the music and ideas of Antonín Dvořák (1841–1904).[18] Her interest in the Bohemian composer, who was a cultural outsider to the German-dominated musical landscape of his day, would have derived partly from his brilliant importing of Bohemian idioms into the German-dominated genres of opera, string quartet, and symphony (a stylistic feature that resonated with her own integration of Black and White idioms). More important, though, would have been the obvious connections between her own career-long promotion of a sense of pride in African American identity in music – in the sense of racial, cultural, and historical memory and preservation that had inspired Joseph M. Trotter's seminal *Music and Some Highly Musical People* already in 1878,[19] and what Joseph Horowitz has called "Dvořák's Prophecy": the 1893 assertion, probably rooting, through Harry T. Burleigh, to Trotter's book, that "the future music of [the United States] must be founded upon what are called the negro melodies," which "must be the real foundation of any serious and original school of composition to be developed in the United States" and which offered "all that is needed for a great and noble school of music."[20] As we shall see, Bonds possessed a strong sense of personal mission and considered it her "Destiny" (upper-case *D*) to "go farther" than those who had preceded her in pursuing that mission. In view of her close relationship to Florence B. Price, whose own connections with Dvořák's music are often noted, and who had echoed Dvořák in her statement that "a national musical idiom" and a truly American folk music existed "in the Negro spirituals,"[21] Bonds's own musical celebration of "the negro melodies" and other Black vernacular styles is probably more than an exploration of her own personal heritage (though it is certainly this as well). It is also a historiographic assertion of self and, because of its deep syncretism of disparate idioms, bolder and more brilliant than anything submitted by Price, Burleigh, William Levi Dawson, R. Nathaniel Dett, or any of Dvořák's other conceptual progeny. The musical contributions of Margaret Bonds offered her contemporaries a remarkable and vivid glimpse of what American classical music might have looked like had Trotter's and Dvořák's vision been heeded rather than pushed aside by what Horowitz calls "the modernist juggernaut" – the mid-twentieth-century trend toward modernism as defining aesthetic stance and, ultimately, arbiter of perceived historical significance in music and the other arts.[22] Now recovered after decades of marginalization, they also open up new possibilities to our own world – and *The Montgomery Variations* and *Credo*, rising from the ideological and social terrain brilliantly mapped by W. E. B. Du Bois, stand as twin summits of the musical syncretism and societal mission she embarked on in her collaboration with Langston Hughes, beckoning us to reach for their heights.

A Note on This Book

The elements of the book are organized with an archlike symmetry modeled on that of Bonds's *Credo*. It is divided into two parts, the first centered on *The Montgomery Variations* and the second centered on the *Credo*. The center line in this bipartite division is straddled by Chapters 2 and 3, which deal with the two compositions from analytical perspectives. Enfolding these, Chapters 1 and 4 discuss the works from primarily contextual viewpoints. Finally, that main body is framed by an Introduction and Epilogue. The Introduction summarizes the major events and issues in Bonds's life, including the issues that she faced as a social activist and Black woman in the turbulent twentieth century. The Epilogue returns to the issue of the deep segregation of concert life in the United States touched on in this Preface and explores a particularly brilliant and audacious gambit that Bonds undertook in these works: during a time of extraordinary heat and violence surrounding gender justice and racial justice, Bonds, an African American woman, solicited the overwhelmingly White male corps of performers who dominated US orchestras to join with her in giving musical voice to expansive and powerful musical celebrations of racial equality, Black music, and the beauty and power of Blackness generally.

This book has been written with an eye to the newness of the *New Cambridge Music Handbooks* series and the broader cultural footprint offered by the series in its reimagined form. These considerations pose an opportunity, but they also necessitate new solutions to issues that did not previously exist. Most obviously, one cannot assume that readers will have the sort of familiarity with, and easy access to, the works that are central to this volume that readers had for the canonical works, most of them in the public domain, that were central to the original Cambridge Music Handbooks series. This means that many examples are necessary in order to illustrate essential points concerning music that remains unfamiliar to most readers. Examples for *The Montgomery Variations* are my own piano reductions based on the full score, and those from the *Credo* are compressed from Margaret Bonds's own piano-vocal score for that work.[23] My thanks to the heirs of Margaret Bonds and Hildegard Publishing Company for permission to use these materials.

A word on terminology is also necessary. Race is a social construct, not a biological one, and in the United States – the home of Margaret Bonds, and of Langston Hughes and W. E. B. Du Bois until Du Bois moved to Ghana in 1961 – it is so nearly synonymous with caste that in popular usage it has all but completely eclipsed the latter.[24] Even so, Bonds, Hughes, and Du Bois all understood race as a phenomenon both social and biological. They never spoke of caste and spoke of what Du Bois called "the darker races" in terminology that has now fallen from use. Because this book adopts a consciously synchronic perspective, it reproduces their verbiage without comment. My own words mirror the insufficiency of the social artifice itself: "Black," "Blacks," "Black folk," and related terms are commonly used in accordance with current parlance, even though the designated persons are of many different shades and colors; "African Americans" denotes Blacks in or of the United States. Readers may sense my discomfort with these terms, all of which are of dubious accuracy and appropriateness at one time or another; for this I can only apologize.

ACKNOWLEDGMENTS

First and foremost, I wish to thank Mr. Orestes Richardson and the heirs of Margaret Bonds for their kind permission to publish my editions of the two works discussed in this book, and for their general stewardship of the legacy of Margaret Bonds. Special thanks also to Hildegard Publishing Company for permission to include music examples based on their editions of those works.[25] I also thank the Booth Family Center for Special Collections at Georgetown University (Washington, DC) for granting access to, and permission to use, the autographs for those two compositions. For access to and permission to use other valuable sources I thank the Beinecke Rare Book and Manuscript Collection at Yale University (New Haven), the Carl Van Vechten Trust, the W. E. B. Du Bois Center at the University of Massachusetts–Amherst, and the Archives and Rare Books Division, Schomburg Center for Research in Black Culture, the New York Public Library. At the University of Colorado–Boulder Libraries, I especially thank Susan R. Thomas, Director of American Music Research Center, and David M. Hays, Archivist of Rare and Distinctive Collections. A great debt of gratitude is due to Heidi Marshall, Head of Archives and Special Collections at Columbia College (Chicago), for her assistance in accessing the priceless materials in the Center for Black Music Research Collection in that library. Special gratitude is due to Charla Burlenda Wilson, Archivist for the Black Experience in the Northwestern University Libraries, and Jason Nargis, Distinctive Collections Librarian at Northwestern University, for assistance in all manner of inquiries pertaining to Northwestern's rich documentation of the life and achievements of Margaret Bonds. To Du Bois scholar Reiland Rabaka, Professor of African, African American, and Caribbean Studies in the Department of Ethnic Studies and founder of the Center for African and African American Studies at the University of Colorado–Boulder, I owe many thanks for assistance in coming to terms with the ever-rich and unceasingly important legacies of W. E. B. Du Bois as they bear on this book. Further thanks for myriad forms of support go to Professor Jonathan Bellman (University of Northern Colorado–Greeley), Professor Frederick Binkholder (Georgetown University), pianist Lara Downes (California), Professor Sandra Jean Graham (Babson College), Professor Anna Harwell Celenza (Johns Hopkins University), Professor Angel Gil-Ordoñez (Georgetown University), Professor Jason Hoogerhyde (Southwestern University), Professor Phil Hopkins (Southwestern University), Joao Martins (University of California–Irvine), Professor Shana Thomas Mashego (George Washington University), Professor Brian Moon (University of Arizona), Professor Alicia L. Moore (Southwestern University), Professor Denise Neary (Royal Irish Academy of Music), Anthony E. Philpott (Raleigh, North Carolina), Professor Douglass Seaton (Florida State University), and Professor Kimberly A. Smith (Southwestern University). For the invitation to contribute this book to the New Cambridge Music Handbooks series I thank Professor Nicole Grimes (University of California–Irvine) and Kate Brett at Cambridge University Press; and for shepherding the book through to completion I thank Nigel Graves, Sharmila Sivaram, and Makenzi Crouch for bringing her expertise to bear in helping the manuscript to live up to its potential. Finally, special thanks go to Cindy Cooper, who has not only been there every step of the way in the conception and creation of this book but also has been a constant source of support, and of patient and insightful feedback. To say that this book would not exist without her is an understatement.

***

I never knew her, never even met her. But if it's true that every book is ultimately a tale of gratitude translated into other terms, then the tale of this book begins with Ms. Ella Mae Long (ca. 1903–91). My mother's recollections of Ella's bravery, wisdom, teaching, and love deep in the Jim Crow South of the 1940s are the earliest stories I remember having heard, and they brought inspiration to my young and uncomprehending heart. Ms. Long was one of those courageous souls, so visionary in so many ways, who participated in the Great Migration. She was born in Anniston,

Acknowledgments

Alabama, worked for a time as a domestic servant in Atlanta, then went on to earn a nursing degree from the Tuskegee Institute and ultimately become head of surgical nurses at People's Hospital in St. Louis – a Black hospital and, in the segregated health care system of the segregated United States until the mid-1960s, the only medical facility in St. Louis that allowed African American physicians and surgeons to treat private patients. My mother was finally able to locate and reconnect with Ms. Long in an eldercare facility near St. Louis in 1990, visiting her several times during the final year of her life. What Ms. Long did after People's Hospital closed in 1978 is unclear, but this much I know: through my mother's stories and the wisdom, strength, and love she taught to her, Ella Long is the soil in which this book roots. My gratitude for the richness of that soil is deep and humble.

Finally, I thank my mother, Mrs. Jacqueline Cooper, the dedicatee of this book, for those stories – for making them a part of my own story and sharing her own wisdom, courage, and love with me.

Notes

1. The term "rediscovery" is most broadly and frequently applied to Florence B. Price, whose music, like Bonds's, is experiencing a significant rebound in public musical life. See for example Alex Ross, "The Rediscovery of Florence Price," *The New Yorker*, Feb. 5, 2018.
2. For example, Bonds's arrangements of the spirituals "He's Got the Whole World in His Hand" and "You Can Tell the World" have remained common in performance, as have her "Three Dream Portraits," "The Negro Speaks of Rivers," and "Troubled Water." Many lexica of African American composers and women composers have mentioned Bonds (e.g., Mildred Denby Green, *Black Women Composers: A Genesis* [Boston, MA: Twayne, 1983]), and she figures in narratives such as Eileen Southern, *The Music of Black Americans: A History*, 3rd ed. (New York: W. W. Norton, 1997). These studies generally repeat the same, necessarily small corpus of basic facts, but an important contribution was made in 2007 with Helen Walker-Hill's *From Spirituals to Symphonies: African American Women Composers and Their Music* (Urbana: University of Illinois Press, 2007), which included a full chapter on Bonds that went beyond anything achieved previously.

Acknowledgments

3. "Recovery" is a more satisfactory word than the popularly used "rediscovery" for several reasons – not least because in order to be "rediscovered," one must first be "discovered," a term that has never been and should never be applied to Bonds, Florence Price, or any of the other usual subjects for whom that term is popularly reserved.
4. At this writing, the best work-list and bibliography of these sources are still those in Helen Walker-Hill's biographical chapter (*From Spirituals to Symphonies*, 172–88).
5. See Anne Midgette, "A Forgotten Voice for Civil Rights Rises in Song at Georgetown," *The Washington Post*, November 10, 2017. On the Georgetown University Bonds papers see also Anna Harwell Celenza, *Margaret Bonds and Langston Hughes: A Musical Friendship* (Washington, DC: Georgetown University Library, 2016).
6. Margaret Bonds, *Credo*, ed. John Michael Cooper (Worcester, MA: Hildegard Publishing, 2020); Bonds, *The Montgomery Variations*, ed. John Michael Cooper (Worcester, MA: Hildegard Publishing, 2020).
7. Margaret Bonds, "Lecture for THE QUEST CLUB," Georgetown University Libraries, Washington, DC, Booth Family Center for Special Collections (shelfmark GTM-130530, Box 18, folder 4), 2.
8. On the Bach revival, see (most generally) Nicholas Temperley and Peter Wollny, "Bach Revival," *Grove Music Online* (2001; accessed September 29, 2021); further, Christine Blanken, "Dokumente der Wiener Bach-Pflege" in *Bach: Beiträge zur Rezeptionsgeschichte, Interpretationsgeschichte und Pädagogik – Drei Symposien im Rahmen des 83. Bachfestes der Neuen Bachgesellschaft in Salzburg 2008: Bericht*, ed. Thomas Hochradner and Ulrich Leisinger (Freiburg im Breisgau: Rombach, 2010), 23–49; Beatrix Borchardt, "Einschreiben in eine männliche Genealogie? Überlegungen zur Bach-Rezeption Fanny Hensels" in *"Zu gross, zu unerreichbar": Bach-Rezeption im Zeitalter Mendelssohns und Schumanns*, ed. Anselm Hartinger, Christoph Wolff, and Peter Wollny (Leipzig: Breitkopf & Härtel, 2007), 59–76; Hans-Joachim Hinrichsen, "Kantatenkomposition in der 'Hauptstadt von Sebastian Bach': Fanny Hensels geistliche Chorwerke und die Berliner Bach-Tradition" in *Fanny Hensel, geb. Mendelssohn Bartholdy: Das Werk*, ed. Martina Helmig (Munich: edition text + kritik, 1997), 115–29; Philip Olleson, "Samuel Wesley and the English Bach Awakening" in *The English Bach Awakening: Knowledge of J. S. Bach and His Music in England (1750–1830)*, ed. Michael Kassler (Aldershot: Ashgate, 2004), 251–313; Christoph Wolff, "Sara Levy's Musical Salon and Her Bach Collection" in *Sara Levy's World: Gender, Judaism, and the Bach Tradition in Enlightenment Berlin*,

ed. Rebecca Cypress and Nancy Sinkoff (Rochester: University of Rochester Press, 2018), 39–51.

9. Margaret Bonds, interview with James Hatch, cited in Ashley Jennifer Jackson, "Margaret Bonds and The Ballad of the Brown King: An Historical Overview and Analysis" (DMA diss., The Juilliard School, 2014), 70.

10. Letter from Bonds (New York) to Hughes (New York), October 1, 1960. Beinecke Rare Book and Manuscript Library, Yale Collection of American Literature, James Weldon Johnson, Langston Hughes papers (shelfmark JWJ 26, Box 16, folder 374: no. 217). Citations to this Collection will henceforth be cited as "Yale JWJ 26," followed by the box number, folder number, and (as applicable) item number within the folder. On Bonds's use of Black musical idioms in *The Ballad of the Brown King*, see especially Jackson, "Margaret Bonds and The Ballad of the Brown King," ch. 15 (pp. 70–80).

11. Bonds's correspondence with Langston Hughes reveals persistent tensions between her and Holt.

12. Lucy Caplan, "'Strange What Cosmopolites Music Makes of Us': Classical Music, the Black Press, and Nora Douglas Holt's Black Feminist Audiotopia," *Journal of the Society for American Music* 14 (2020): 308–36.

13. Caplan, "Strange What Cosmopolites," 309.

14. Caplan, "Strange What Cosmopolites," esp. 324–25.

15. Yale JWJ 26, Box 16, folder 370: no. 20. For more information on this letter and the play that prompted it, see Ch. 1, p. 24–26.

16. W. E. Burghardt Du Bois, *The Souls of Black Folk: Essays and Sketches*, 3rd ed. (Chicago: A. C. McClurg, 1903), 250–64.

17. See Portia K. Maultsby, *Afro-American Religious Music: A Study in Musical Diversity*, Papers of the Hymn Society of America 35 (Springfield, OH: The Hymn Society of America, 1981); further Shana Thomas Mashego, "Music from the Soul of Woman: The Influence of the African American Presbyterian and Methodist Traditions on the Classical Compositions of Florence Price and Dorothy Rudd Moore" (DMA diss., University of Arizona, 2010).

18. See n. 2 in Chapter 4 for more information regarding the Northwestern University music-history curriculum during Bonds's time there.

19. James M. Trotter, *Music and Some Highly Musical People: Containing Brief Chapters on I. A Description of Music. II. The Music of Nature. III. A Glance at the History of Music. IV. The Power, Beauty, and Uses of Music. Following Which Are Given Sketches of the Lives of Remarkable Musicians of the Colored Race. With Portraits, and an Appendix Containing Copies of*

Music Composed by Colored Men (Boston, MA: Lee and Shepard, 1878).

20. See Joseph Horowitz, *Dvořák's Prophecy and the Vexed Fate of Black Classical Music* (New York: W. W. Norton, 2021), 1–9, esp. 7–8. As Horowitz points out (p. 205), Michael Beckerman has shown that this article was probably authored by James Creelman.

21. See Douglas W. Shadle, *Antonín Dvořák's New World Symphony* (New York: Oxford University Press, 2021), 159.

22. Horowitz, *Dvořák's Prophecy*, 202.

23. Bonds wrote the vocal parts in four separate staves, but this book compresses these into two staves instead. In the *Credo* examples, the vocal parts follow the latest authorized version – i.e., they are given as in the autograph full orchestral score housed in the Booth Family Center for Special Collections in the Georgetown University Library – while the piano part is taken from Bonds's autograph piano part.

24. See, most recently, Isabel Wilkerson, *Caste: The Origins of Our Discontents* (New York: Random House, 2020).

25. Margaret Bonds, *Credo* (piano-vocal score, full score, and parts available for rental through Theodore Presser), ed. John Michael Cooper (Worcester, MA: Hildegard Publishing, 2020); Margaret Bonds, *The Montgomery Variations* (score and parts available for rental through Theodore Presser), ed. John Michael Cooper (Worcester, MA: Hildegard Publishing, 2020); Margaret Bonds, *Credo* (piano-vocal score, octavo), ed. John Michael Cooper (Worcester, MA: Hildegard Publishing, 2022); Margaret Bonds, "Especially Do I Believe in the Negro Race" (*Credo*, No. 2), ed. John Michael Cooper (Worcester, MA: Hildegard Publishing, 2022); Margaret Bonds, *I Believe* ("Especially Do I Believe in the Negro Race," from *Credo*), ed. John Michael Cooper, arr. for piano solo by Lara Downes (Worcester, MA: Hildegard Publishing, 2023); Margaret Bonds, *Credo* (study score), ed. John Michael Cooper (Worcester, MA: Hildegard Publishing, 2023).

INTRODUCTION

This book is a specimen of polyphony. Through the two works that are its subject, we can hear the voice of Margaret Allison Bonds (1913–72): composer, pianist, Black feminist, racial-justice warrior, humanitarian. Through these musical utterances, her voice in turn enables us to hear the voices of her distinguished collaborators and sources of inspiration – voices that include W. E. B. Du Bois, Langston Hughes, Adele Addison, Betty Allen, Will Marion Cook, Abbie Mitchell, and Leontyne Price, among others. Through them, too, we hear the voices of millions of other participants in the great racial-justice movements of the twentieth century in America and beyond. *The Montgomery Variations* and *Credo* of Margaret Bonds not only enable us to understand the historical roots of these movements and the lived experiences and ideas, aspirations and hopes and sufferings of their participants, but also empower us to recognize those movements' affinities to our own time and the pressing need for latter-day folk to (as the composer herself put it) "go farther."[1]

In order to provide a framework for that polyphony, this Introduction begins by summarizing each of the societal currents that made up those social-justice movements and explaining how these developments connected to the life and work of the composer of *The Montgomery Variations* and *Credo*. This done, it then more directly connects those contextual notes to the personal and professional circumstances that inspired those two works, offering a brief, thematically organized summary of the upbringing, education, and career of Margaret Bonds.

The Great Migration

In 1903, W. E. B. Du Bois (1867–1963), whose 1904 *Credo* would provide the text for the largest choral composition of Margaret Bonds in the mid-1960s, famously declared that "the problem of the Twentieth Century is the problem of the color-line."[2] This prophetic observation was born of Du Bois's pioneering sociological observations of Black–White relations in the world around him and the post-Reconstruction era, as well as his documentation and understanding of the transatlantic slave trade, slavery, and post-Civil War White subjugation of Blacks in the United States (memorialized through the notorious Jim Crow system and granted a specious veneer of legal validity through court cases such as *Plessy v. Ferguson*), and the emergent exodus of Southern Blacks to the urban North. After 1906, however, he came increasingly under the sway of the thinking of distinguished Columbia University anthropologist Frans Boas (1858–1942), who definitively refuted claims for a biological basis for scientific racism and, in a powerful commencement speech given at Du Bois's own Atlanta University, documented sub-Saharan Africa's primordial contributions to ancient civilization and to world culture generally.[3] The realization of the predominant White culture's erasure of these contributions from historical narratives, and consequent suppression (or theft) of Blacks' distinguished history and heritage,[4] combined with the sociologist Du Bois's understanding that the "White" populations who, especially since the Berlin Congo Congress of 1884, exercised colonial, economic, legal, and military dominance over peoples of color in Africa and Asia actually constituted a minority of the world population.[5] To the end of his life, then, he argued that the color line was not entirely an American phenomenon, as many initially construed it, but rather a global one – what he termed "the world color line." A pan-African alliance of peoples of color worldwide, collectively rejecting these tools of White dominance, was the key to global equality in its purest possible form.

The urban concentrations of diasporic populations of color that were made possible by the mass exodus of Blacks from the sharecropping, peonage, and Black Codes of the Jim Crow South were a crucial step in the direction of this quest for racial-justice and anti-colonialist global equality, for they offered migrant Blacks a sense of collective identity and solidarity that were systemically denied them in the geographically dispersed rural environs of the South. Even though formerly enslaved Southern Blacks had worked their entire lives for no wages and with no education or property through the Civil War (1861–65), and thus had no viable capital to put toward the cost of a relocation across hundreds of miles, they began abandoning their former enslavers' lands and moving north already in the 1870s: between 1870 and 1910 some 410,000 Blacks emigrated from the South to the North, the West, and Canada, leaving behind the brutal oppression and deprivation of the former slave states and seeking education, family, opportunity, work, and a fresh start.[6] Those figures surged after about 1915 as the White-on-Black violence, anti-Black culture, and disfranchisement at the ballot box of the South worsened, even as the demand for munitions for use in World War I offered new, previously unthinkable opportunities for employment in the North, and with it education and enfranchisement. Between 1919 and 1970, an estimated six million Blacks migrated. While some of this movement was cyclical, from rural to urban areas within the South (especially Atlanta, Georgia; Charleston, North Carolina; Dallas, Texas; and Memphis, Tennessee), most of it was from the South to the North, the West, or Canada. Over time, this exodus devastated the Southern economy and transformed the map of Black life beyond the former Mason–Dixon line.[7] The migrants' paths to the nearest and best destinations were guided in part by the Eastern seaboard and major rivers, but they were also guided by the very railroads whose segregational practices were one of the hated symbols of the Jim Crow South. The six most important destination cities were Chicago, Detroit, Los Angeles, New York, Philadelphia, and St. Louis. In a touch of beautifully poetic irony, those rail lines and the Southern sufferings they symbolized were memorialized by migrants to these metropolises in literature, music (especially spirituals and the blues), and the visual arts – so that in the arts the hated segregated rail lines became, in the words of Farrah Griffin, "a symbol of escape to freedom."[8]

As we shall see, Margaret Bonds enjoyed strong ties to most of these municipal symbols of freedom reclaimed. She was born, raised, and educated in Chicago; frequently traveled to Detroit; was a favorite in the music pages of the African American press in Philadelphia; was based in New York for most of the period 1939–67; and spent extensive time in Los Angeles. As an African American woman, she knew that freedom from the Jim Crow South was a far cry from true freedom. Her native Chicago, founded by a Black man, Jean Baptiste Point du Sable (1745–1818), was also home to one of the early twentieth century's most notorious race riots (in 1919, when she was six years old) and was firmly segregated. White Chicagoans' "restrictive covenants" meant that African Americans had to live in the metropolis's "Black Belt" on the south side – an area that was publicly (and not misleadingly) promoted as home to "race" culture and enterprise, but whose economy was equally or more driven by the illegal lottery known as "policy" and other criminal enterprises, as well as the thriving entertainment district known as the Stroll (where Bonds's friend and mentor Florence Price worked for a time shortly after her move to Chicago[9]).

New York's Harlem is usually cited as the most important destination of Southern Blacks in the Great Migration, but Chicago was arguably an even more important magnet for Black solidarity and community, for it was home to an integrated movie theater, a high school that hired Black teachers, and, perhaps most importantly, the *Chicago Defender*, the first African American newspaper to achieve a readership of more than 100,000, which was covertly distributed in the South and intrepid in its denunciations of the South and its promotion of the North (especially Chicago) as a land of promise and opportunity.[10] As Du Bois had foreseen, the demographic concentration of communities of color, for all its privations, also produced cultural, economic, and political solidarity, so that Chicago's painful segregation and vice laid the seed for a lifelong commitment to social justice and an ethos of racial uplift in the creative imagination of the young and brilliant Margaret Bonds.

One telling indication of this socially conscious artistic commitment on Bonds's part was the penchant for collaborative creation

4

that she displayed throughout her career. Another – dating from just weeks before the second Southern tour that would complete the inspiration for *The Montgomery Variations* – was a ballet for which she composed the score (now lost) many years later. The work was written for the dance company of African American choreographer and dancer Talley Beatty (1918–95), a protégé of Katherine Dunham who, like Bonds, grew up in Chicago. Known for "coolly empathetic portraits of inner-city life and for high-energy, technically demanding jazz innovations,"[11] Beatty on March 7, 1964, staged a production with music by Bonds that "show[ed] the Negro, first in Africa, then on the slave block, and finally caught up in other incidents of racial injustice."[12] Response was lukewarm, but the work as a whole reflects Bonds's enduring cognizance of the intersection of racial injustice and Black creative solidarity.

Its title: *The Migration.*

Black Renaissances: Harlem, Chicago, Los Angeles

One effect of the Great Migration predicted by Du Bois was the great flowering of African American cultural production that resulted when Black folk gathered together in a spirit of creative community and solidarity. The prediction is important because of its consilience with Du Bois's pan-Africanist agenda and its assertion of the oneness of art, economics, politics, and society as a whole – for its affirmation of the power and dignity of a Black creative imagination that the dominant-caste non-Black rulers of the world strove mightily to suppress and deny.

It is also important, though, for the ways in which it departs from much of Du Bois's other work. Much of Du Bois's training and work as an empirical sociologist led him to geographically and politically focused inquiries and conclusions ("The Negroes of Farmville, Virginia: A Social Study," 1898; *The Philadelphia Negro: A Social Study*, 1899; *The Georgia Negro: A Social Study*, 1900; etc.); this aspect of his work, together with his understanding of the extraordinary individualized diversity of Black folk and peoples of color generally, was central to the prophetic intersectionality and resistance to what Reiland Rabaka has termed "epistemic apartheid" that characterized much of his thinking.[13] But the flourishing of Black cultural production that he predicted, and worked to achieve, as a result of the resettlement of millions of Black folk into communities was not geographically, culturally, or politically particularized. Rather, Du Bois's vision for non-White diasporic people's cultural renaissance was of a supranational, indeed global nature, one that would transcend the historical subjugation of what he called "the darker races" and their cultures – effectively emancipating, internationally, a facet of human creativity that had been both suppressed and denied.

As is well known, the separately named "Black renaissances" of the twentieth century – the "Harlem renaissance," "Black Chicago renaissance," and so on – were so named only after the fact and were, for much of the twentieth century, considered part of a larger "New Negro" movement. In effectively creating these separate historiographic articulations of what contemporary contributors and observers such as Du Bois and Alain Locke considered a single multifaceted cultural movement,[14] the voluminous scholarship on the "Black renaissances" of the twentieth century has created anachronistic narratives of geographically particularized cultural flowerings, each of which eventually failed or faded: the Harlem Renaissance is discussed as a phenomenon chronologically as well as geographically discrete from the Black Chicago Renaissance, and both are portrayed as things that ultimately failed, yielding to what became the West Coast Black Renaissance. These portrayals are misleading in their depictions of these proliferations of Black cultural production as overlapping but ultimately separate and, in some sense, competing phenomena rather than facets of a long and overarching Black cultural renaissance that manifested itself in not just Harlem, Chicago, and Los Angeles but also Detroit, Philadelphia, Pittsburgh, St. Louis, and dozens of other urban areas – and is ongoing still today. They also assert a series of narratives of failure where a narrative of expansion and prodigious growth is appropriate. If we set aside these anachronistic narratives of failure and recognize the extraordinary Black cultural production of the twentieth century on its own terms, then we can not only dispense with the implied inadequacy and negativity that inevitably result when commentators assign more-or-less arbitrary endings to events still ongoing, while acknowledging the vital air of community and cultural solidarity that existed among the participants in, and observers of, that flourishing. Acknowledging that the boundaries between, for instance, the "Harlem Renaissance" and the "Black Chicago Renaissance" are anachronistic historiographic artifices in turn also enables us to glimpse the freedom of the many and varied currents and cross-currents entailed in the robust exchange of art, letters, literature, and music among these cities and the movement of newly affluent Black folk among those locales.[15]

The benefits to such a rethinking are many. By declining to create artificial aesthetic distinctions and contradictions where only variations existed, we can acknowledge the various geographic iterations of this cultural flourishing as an ongoing collective moment when (to borrow Carolyn Denard's characterization of the Harlem iteration) "the creative arts, *not* economic determinism, *nor* political strategy, *nor* constitutional rhetoric, *nor* military strength, but the *arts* were believed to be an agent through which individuals could effect social change" (emphasis original).[16] Further, in recognizing that assertion of artistic agency in social change, we can acknowledge the shared emphasis on racial and gender justice that characterized all these flourishings and the role that all played in laying the foundation for the mature Civil Rights Movement. And to make these movements concretely relevant to the focal points of this book: the Civil Rights Movement, which was a rebellion against the Jim Crow South and an extension of the long Black cultural renaissance, is a movement whose articulated beginning is generally considered to be the Montgomery bus boycott (1955–56), which, as we shall see, was the principal inspiration for Margaret Bonds's *Montgomery Variations*.

Margaret Bonds and the Imperative of Social Justice through Art

This view of the several geographic iterations of an overarching Black cultural renaissance rooted in the desire for social change and directly connected to the Civil Rights Movement concurs with the geography of Margaret Bonds's creative life. She was born and raised in Chicago and began her career there; spent most of her life

7

based in Harlem; had two important stays in Los Angeles (1942–43 and 1967–72); and traveled frequently among the other urban areas that were the principal sites of Black cultural production. In addition to the two Southern tours that led directly to *The Montgomery Variations* and indirectly to the *Credo*, she maintained extensive connections with major Southern cultural hubs, including Atlanta, Fisk University (Nashville, Tennessee), and the Hampton Institute (Hampton, Virginia). Her work as a solo and collaborative pianist addressed itself to vernacular and cultivated tastes, stereotypically Black and stereotypically White ones alike. Her letters and musical compositions reveal a keen appetite for poetry and for literature generally, and her music reflects an extraordinary fluency in virtually every style and genre of her day, a stylistic versatility that defied conventional barriers of race and caste. And through it all the ideas of artists and the arts as agents of social change, of giving voice to the voiceless, affirmation to the oppressed, and inspiration to the hopeless ran like a red thread.

Margaret Bonds's forty-two-year career as social-justice advocate was inculcated in her by her parents. Her father, Monroe Alpheus Majors (1864–1960), a medical doctor originally from Texas who practiced in Texas, California, and Illinois, was a lifelong activist and advocate for Black folk generally and Black women especially – an intersectional advocacy that is clearly mirrored in Margaret Bonds's own life and work.[17] He grew up in Reconstruction and during that short spell of new prospects for Black folk served as a page in the Texas state legislature – but had to flee the state in the aftermath, when White-against-Black violence spiraled. He established a medical association for Black doctors (who were not allowed in the American Medical Association) and, after moving to Los Angeles in 1888, became the first African American to practice medicine west of the Rocky Mountains. He was an associate of Frederick Douglass and a longtime friend of Paul Laurence Dunbar. He also wrote for African American newspapers and authored one of the first published books for Black children, the 1893 lexicon *Noted Negro Women: Their Triumphs and Activities* (Jackson, TN: M.V. Lynk). The preface to that volume, the title page of which asserts that "the highest mark of our prosperity, and the strongest proofs of Negro capacity to master the sciences and fine arts, are evinced by the advanced positions to which Negro women have attained," contains words that might well have been written by his daughter, who would be born twenty years later:

> The world is full of books, yet few of them appeal directly and peculiarly to the Negro race. Many ... have their beginning and ending in fancy, without special design for the elevation of mind or the culture of literary taste and pure morals, but for entertainment and amusement and gratification of sentiment without utility to the reader in any sense whatsoever. We commend [the following] pages to the reading world, trusting that they will for long stand out in bold relief, a signification of Negro progress.[18]

Although Margaret Bonds would later write that her father had "great intellect" and could have been "a great man had he not tried to conform to the taboos, inhibitions and the rest of them,"[19] she apparently was never close to him; her parents separated when she was two, and the marriage was annulled when she was six.[20] Instead, her correspondence makes clear that she revered her mother, Estella C. Bonds (1882–1957), who taught her music and the importance of advancing the welfare of Black folk through education, music, and the arts generally.[21] Educated at Chicago Musical College, Estella Bonds was the longtime organist at Chicago's historic Berean Baptist Church, a charter member of the National Association of Negro Musicians, and a founding faculty member of the city's Coleridge-Taylor School of Music. Her modest home on the south side of the segregated city hosted weekly salons and was a frequent haunt of Black artistic notables – among them Bonds's composition teacher Will Marion Cook (1869–1944); poet Countee Cullen (1903–46); composer William Levi Dawson (1899–1990); soprano Lillian Evanti (1890–1967); soprano, actress, and activist Abbie Mitchell (1884–1960; eventual dedicatee of Bonds's *Credo*[22]); longtime friend, collaborator, and literary icon Langston Hughes (1902–67); friend, mentor, and early teacher Florence B. Price (1887–1953); and playwright, jazz composer, and bandleader Noble Sissle (1889–1975). Recalling (with some obvious exaggeration) that through the many visits to her childhood home she "had actual physical contact with all the living composers of African descent," she went on to characterize Estella Bonds's cultivation among Black artists in biblical terms:

My mother had a collector's nose for anything that was artistic, and, a true woman of God, she lived the Sermon on the Mount. Her loaves and fish fed a multitude of pianists, singers, violinists and composers, and those who were not in need of material food came for spiritual food. Under her wings many a musician trusted, and she was my link with the Lord.[23]

As we shall see, this upbringing left a deep impression on Margaret Bonds; her letters make clear that her sense of indebtedness to these personalities and their art, and to her own ancestors, gave her a pronounced sense of *Destiny* (her word; uppercase *D* original) that played out in her life and work in countless ways. That need for achievement led to successes already in grade school: she won piano scholarships to Chicago Musical College at ages eight and nine and later scholarships from the Coleridge-Taylor School of Music. Her undergraduate degree at prestigious Northwestern University was made possible by scholarships from the intercollegiate, historically African American sorority Alpha Kappa Alpha and the National Association of Negro Musicians, and at the age of seventeen she achieved the distinction of giving the premiere of Florence Price's first (E-minor) *Fantasie nègre* at the national meeting of the National Association of Negro Musicians.[24] This distinction was to be augmented by her winning the Best Song prize in the national Rodman Wanamaker Competition in Musical Composition for Composers of the Negro Race in 1932, performing what was probably a piano-duet arrangement of Price's E-minor *Fantasie nègre* as accompaniment to a ballet premiere of that work by Katherine Dunham and the Modern Dancers in December 1932,[25] becoming the first Black pianist to perform with the Chicago Symphony Orchestra (at the *Century of Progress* World's Fair on June 15, 1933), and performing the same work with the Woman's Symphony Orchestra of Chicago on October 12, 1934.[26] Her master's degree was funded by a scholarship from the Julius Rosenwald Foundation. Although Bonds was never shy about expressing her gratitude to Northwestern and was awarded one of the University's alumni Merit Awards in 1967, the overwhelming Whiteness of the institution and its curriculum (i.e., its paucity of students and faculty of color and lack of representation of Black figures in its courses) and the harsh racism she faced while there contrasted sharply with her firsthand knowledge of Black achievement – and certainly helped to motivate her lifelong remedial work in this regard. Her remarks on a play put on there in 1937 reflect this conflict,[27] but the sharpest indication of the lasting presence of the pain caused by that educational segregation is her description of its contrast with the effect on her of Langston Hughes's poem *The Negro Speaks of Rivers*:

I was in this prejudiced university, this terribly prejudiced place. . . . I was looking in the basement of the Evanston Public Library where they had the poetry. I came in contact with this wonderful poem, "The Negro Speaks of Rivers," and I'm sure it helped my feelings of security. Because in that poem he [Langston Hughes] tells how great the black man is. And if I had any misgivings, which I would have to have – here you are in a setup where the restaurants won't serve you and you're going to college, you're sacrificing, trying to get through school – and I know that poem helped save me.[28]

Margaret Bonds's understanding of the deep connections between education and racial advocacy resulted in her founding of the Allied Arts Academy in 1938, two years after she and Langston Hughes had befriended one another and one year before she would leave Chicago. The Academy held its opening reception on January 23, 1938, and gave its final concert on June 18, 1939, not long before Bonds relocated to New York. Though not explicitly for Black students, the Academy was located in the Alexander Building at 6407 South Parkway in Chicago's Black Belt and thus intended primarily for Black students. It was a local enterprise but was also announced in the *Detroit Tribune*:

MARGARET A. BONDS, the very talented Chicago Miss who holds several degrees in music and can play the piano like no-body's-business, invited Chicago's fashionables to attend the opening of her new school of dramatics, music and dancing. The name of her studio is the Allied Arts Academy and [it] is located on the second floor of the Alexander Building out South Parkway. . . . Her suite is done in light colors and the piano's done in white. . . . A staff of University trained teachers will carry out the program. . . .

So on Sunday we siped [sic] tea and listened to a very entertaining and inspiring musical program.[29]

The Allied Arts Academy lasted only for the duration of Bonds's stay in Chicago, but she reportedly intended to open a New York branch of the enterprise after moving there.[30] Despite its short existence, it apparently made an impression. Its penultimate concert, given on April 30, 1939, was noted by the Associated Negro Press and attended by reporters from the *Chicago Tribune*, *Chicago Daily News*, and *Chicago Herald-Examiner*. The *Pittsburgh Courier* ran a sizable story by Etta Moten [Barmett] (1901–2004), a celebrated contralto famously identified with the role of Bess in *Porgy and Bess*, about the concert that reflects the young Margaret Bonds's growing national recognition:

"What becomes of the child prodigies?" Do they make good when put to a real test where constant study is required? These are questions which psychologists have been debating in recent years. Chicago music lovers heard the answer Sunday afternoon, when [the] Allied Arts Academy presented Chicago's own Margaret Bonds in a piano recital at Curtiss Hall of the Fine Arts Building in Chicago's Loop.

Critics from the Chicago Tribune, Chicago Daily News, [and] Daily-Examiner, were there to review the concert of a pianist whom they had heard of only when she played with the Illinois Symphony Orchestra [sic] and the Women's Symphony Orchestra. Many members of old Chicago families were there to hear the daughter of Estella Bonds perform. They were reminiscent of the days when at six years of age, she performed at the Coleridge-Taylor School of Music, of which her mother was co-founder. . . .

Miss Bonds is now president and founder of Allied Arts Academy at 6407 South Parkway. Hers was the fourth concert of this season's concert series. . . . Truly the child prodigy has not only grown up, but has worked every step of the way.[31]

Reportedly at the urging of Langston Hughes, Bonds moved to New York "with $37 in her pocket" late in 1939 and there "played all sorts of gigs, wrote ensembles, played rehearsal music and did any chief cook and bottle washer job just so [she] could be honest and do what [she] wanted."[32] Soon, however, she was again at work as art and education advocate and social justice activist. By the spring of 1956 she had founded the Margaret Bonds Chamber Music Society, a group of African American performers whose stated purpose was "to perpetuate and inspire a greater public awareness of the remarkable contributions of Negro composers and poets."[33] In addition to organizing and giving concerts that would promote the music of Black composers, she served on the board of directors of the Waltann School of Creative Arts in New York. She was an active public speaker: her correspondence and other documents record performances, lecture-recitals, and speeches at the American Committee of Jewish Writers, Artists, and Scientists, the National Association of Negro Musicians, the New York State Commission against Discrimination, the QUEST Club of New York, the United Negro College Fund, YMCA and YWCA branches, historically Black colleges and universities, and other venues that were centered on poor areas, persecuted groups, and communities of color of all income brackets.[34] In 1962 she also gave a brief speech at the Madison (New Jersey) campus of Fairleigh Dickinson University titled "Careers in Music Available to Women" – and the text of this speech, while resolutely avoiding obviously negative perspectives, reveals her awareness of the stymieing sexism of the vocations of music.[35] From her 1967 move to Los Angeles to her death, she taught piano lessons and served as music director for the Inner City Institute in that city, also supervising the music for their production of *West Side Story* and composing a new score for a production titled *Burlesque Is Alive*. Her activities demonstrate that social-justice and advocacy groups of many sorts sought (and found) in Margaret Bonds an articulate, engaging, and passionate advocate for their cause.

Equally tellingly, there is a noticeable difference in the programming of Bonds's own recitals from the 1950s on. The surviving programs and press reports show that her repertoire as a college student consisted almost exclusively of works by male composers, most of them European (J. S. Bach, Debussy, and Robert Schumann figure most prominently, but there are also compositions by Brahms, Dohnanyi, Franck, Milhaud, Mozart, Ravel, Domenico Scarlatti, and Tartini); the only exceptions to this rule were infrequent performances of her own works (the recently published *African Dance* on a text by Hughes, *The Negro Speaks of Rivers*, and "Poème d'autonne"[36]). Beginning in the 1940s and early 1950s, however, her own music and works of other Black composers, most prominently Harry Burleigh,

Samuel Coleridge-Taylor, and Florence Price, as well as Bonds's arrangements of spirituals, become more prominent. Music by Black composers never predominates except in the relatively few programs with a theme of "the Negro in music," but the programming clearly positions Black composers as coequal peers of canonical White men and fully entitled participants in the musical space, rather than Black incursions into White space.

Most important, though, is that while Langston Hughes, whose work consistently gave frank and often inspiring voice to Black experience, had been the prevalent poet in her vocal oeuvre since 1936, beginning around 1942 Bonds's own compositions became increasingly explicit in their foregrounding and envoicing of texts and poets that deal with Black ideas, Black experience, and Black history. This increase is particularly marked in her published works. During this period she achieves her distinctive approach to arranging spirituals (e.g., the *Creek-Freedmen Spirituals* [New York: Mutual Music, 1946]), and the press release for her 1947 tour reported that she was "busy working on the score and script for a Broadway show which will set something of a precedent in better race relations when it is produced."[37] But the completion of the first version of *The Ballad of the Brown King* in 1954 dramatically increased the prevalence of this theme in her compositions. That project set the stage for a series of increasingly ambitious "project[ions of] her own people" (as one caption put it[38]) that would lead, seemingly inexorably, to *The Montgomery Variations* and Bonds's setting of the W. E. B. Du Bois *Credo*.

Notes

1. Letter from Bonds to Larry Richardson, December 17, 1942, Booth Family Center for Special Collections, Georgetown University Libraries, Margaret Bonds Papers (shelfmark GTM-130530, Box 2, folder 3). Citations to this collection will henceforth be cited as "Georgetown University Bonds Papers," followed by the shelfmark, box number, and folder number.
2. W. E. Burghardt Du Bois, *The Souls of Black Folk: Essays and Sketches*, 3rd ed. (Chicago: A. C. McClurg, 1903), vii.
3. See David Levering Lewis, *W.E.B. Du Bois: Biography of a Race, 1868–1919* (New York: Henry Holt, 1993), 351–52; further, Julia

E. Liss, "Diasporic Identities: The Science and Politics of Race in the Work of Frans Boas and W. E. B. Du Bois, 1894–1919," *Cultural Anthropology* 13 (1998): 127–66; and Rosemary Levy Zumwalt and William Shedrick Willis, "Franz Boas and W.E.B. Du Bois at Atlanta University, 1906," *Transactions of the American Philosophical Society* 98 (2008): 1–83.

4. This theme would play out in Bonds's and Langston Hughes's cantatas *The Ballad of the Brown King* and *Simon Bore the Cross*; see Chapter 1.
5. See W. E. B. Du Bois, "The African Roots of the War," in David Levering Lewis, *W.E.B. Du Bois: A Reader* (New York: Henry Holt, 1995), 642–51.
6. See Carole Marks, "Black Workers and the Great Migration North," *Phylon (1960–)* 46 (1985): 148–61 at 148.
7. See Stewart E. Tolnay and E. M. Beck, "Rethinking the Role of Racial Violence in the Great Migration," in *Black Exodus: The Great Migration from the American South*, ed. Alferdteen Harrison (Jackson, MS: University Press of Mississippi, 1991), 20–35; Neil R. McMillen, "The Migration and Black Protest in Jim Crow Mississippi," in Harrison, *Black Exodus*, 83–100; Isabel Wilkerson, *The Warmth of Other Suns: The Epic Story of America's Great Migration* (New York: Random House, 2010); Carol Anderson, "Derailing the Great Migration," in her *White Rage: The Unspoken Truth of Our Racial Divide* (New York: Bloomsbury, 2016), 39–66; and Marcus Anthony Hunter and Zandria F. Robinson, *Chocolate Cities: The Black Map of American Life* (Oakland: University of California Press, 2018).
8. Farah Jasmine Griffin, *"Who Set You Flowin'?" The African-American Migration Narrative* (Oxford: Oxford University Press, 1995), 30.
9. Rae Linda Brown, *The Heart of a Woman: The Life and Music of Florence B. Price*, ed. Guthrie P. Ramsey, Jr. (Urbana: University of Illinois Press, 2020), 99.
10. Davarian L. Baldwin, *Chicago's New Negroes: Modernity, the Great Migration, & Black Urban Life* (Chapel Hill: University of North Carolina Press, 2007), 13–15.
11. Jennifer Dunning, "Talley Beatty, 76, a Leader in Lyrical Jazz Choreography," *New York Times* (May 1, 1995).
12. Allen Hughes, "Dance: Beatty Company," *New York Times* (March 9, 1964).
13. See especially Reiland Rabaka, *Against Epistemic Apartheid: W.E.B. Du Bois and the Disciplinary Decadence of Sociology* (Lanham, MD: Lexington Books, 2010); and Rabaka, "'The Damnation of Women': Critique of Patriarchy, Contributions to Black Feminism, and Early

Intersectionality," in his *Du Bois: A Critical Introduction* (Cambridge: Polity Press, 2021), 95–120.

14. See Alain Locke, "Harlem," *The Survey Graphic* 53 (1925): 629–30 at 629.
15. See Ernest Julius Mitchell II, "'Black Renaissance': A Brief History of the Concept," *Amerikastudien/America Studies* 55 (2010): 641–65.
16. Carolyn C. Denard, "Afterword," in *The Harlem Renaissance Reexamined: A Revised and Expanded Edition*, ed. Victor A. Kramer and Robert A. Russ (Troy, NY: The Whitson Publishing Company, 1998), 375–82 at 378.
17. The following biographical information on Monroe Majors is adapted from W. Montague Cobb, "Monroe Alpheus Majors, 1864–," *Journal of the National Medical Association* 47, no. 2 (1955): 139–41. The topic of Margaret Bonds's own Black feminism, briefly discussed in Chapter 3 of this book, is one of the most pressing desiderata of future Bonds research.
18. M[onroe] A[lpheus] Majors, *Noted Negro Women: Their Triumphs and Activities* (Chicago, IL: Donohue & Henneberry, 1893), x.
19. Margaret Bonds (Los Angeles) to Larry Richardson (New York), December 17, 1942 (Georgetown University Bonds Papers, shelfmark GTM-130530, Box 2, folder 3). This letter is discussed in greater detail in Chapter 1.
20. The Bonds–Majors separation is reported in Helen Walker-Hill, "Margaret Bonds," in her *From Spirituals to Symphonies: African-American Women Composers and Their Music* (Westport, CT: Greenwood, 2002), 141–88 at 146. Walker-Hill reports that the couple divorced in 1917, but this is incorrect. The marriage had been annulled "recently" in midsummer 1919 by Judge Charles M. Walker of the Cook County Circuit Court, according to a report of June 21, 1919 in the Chicago newspaper *The Broad Ax* (p. 4), which regularly reported on Estella Bonds's activities.
21. The essentials of Bonds's biography are summarized in Walker-Hill, "Margaret Bonds," 141–58.
22. Bonds later recalled that it was from Mitchell that she "learned the importance of the marriage between words and music which is demanded if one is to have a song of any consequence." See Margaret Bonds, "A Reminiscence," in *The Negro in Music and Art*, ed. Lindsay Patterson (New York: International Library of Negro Life and History, 1967), 190–93 at 190.
23. Bonds, "Reminiscence," 192.
24. Carl Diton, "Musicians Association to Organize Juniors: Hoosier Elected Head," *The Pittsburgh Courier* (September 6, 1930): 5.
25. See Samantha Hannah Oboakorevue Ege, "The Aesthetics of Florence Price: Negotiating the Dissonances of a New World Nationalism" (PhD diss., University of York, 2020), 140–41.

26. See Rae Linda Brown, *The Heart of a Woman: The Life and Music of Florence B. Price*, ed. Guthrie P. Ramsey, Jr. (Urbana: University of Illinois Press, 2020), 158–60.
27. See Chapter 1 (pp. 24–26).
28. Margaret Bonds, taped interview with James Hatch, December 28, 1971, quoted from Walker-Hill, *From Spirituals to Symphonies*, 156.
29. Ulysses W. Botken, "Bulletin Board," *The Detroit Tribune* (January 29, 1938): 6.
30. On November 5, 1939, *The Birmingham News*, describing Bonds as "talented musician, formerly of Chicago, now in New York City," identified her as "director of Allied Arts Academy, of Chicago" and reported that she "plan[ned] opening a branch in New York City" (*The Birmingham News*, November 5, 1939: 24).
31. Etta Moten, "Margaret Bonds, Pianist, in Concert," *The Pittsburgh Courier* (May 6, 1939): 8.
32. Christina Demaitre, "She Has a Musical Mission: Developing Racial Harmony; Heritage Motivates Composing Career," *The Washington Post 87*, no. 253 (August 14, 1964): C2.
33. *The New York Age* (October 20, 1956): 16. The group and its aspirations were introduced in a *New York Age* article titled "Chamber Music Program to Honor H. T. Burleigh" (*New York Age*, October 13, 1956: 21). The Society's members were Bonds (pianist and director), Naomi Pettigrew (soprano), Ida Johnson (alto), Laurence Watson (tenor), Eugene Brice (baritone), and the Marion Cumbo String Quartette.
34. Many letters, programs, press reports, and other documents pertaining to these activities are preserved in the Margaret Bonds Papers of the Booth Family Center for Special Collections, Georgetown University, Washington, DC (shelfmark GTM 130530).
35. "Music Careers for Femmes Is Topic of Pianist Composer at University," *Daily Record*, Long Branch, New Jersey (March 22, 1962): 7. The program for this conference (titled *The Executive Woman*) survives in the Langston Hughes (Yale JWJ 26, Box 16, folder 377: no. 334). The text of this speech survives in the Georgetown University Bonds Papers (shelfmark GTM 130530 Box 5, folder 7).
36. Margaret Bonds, *African Dance*, ed. John Michael Cooper (Worcester, MA: Hildegard Publishing, 2022); Bonds, *The Negro Speaks of Rivers*, 1936 (New York: W.C. Handy, 1942); Bonds, "Poème d'autonne," 1934, in *Rediscovering Margaret Bonds: Art Songs, Spirituals, Musical Theater and Popular Songs*, ed. Louise Toppin (Ann Arbor, MI: Videmus, 2021), 42–45.
37. "Noted Composer-Pianist to Star in Broadway Show," *Alabama Tribune, Montgomery, Alabama* (July 18, 1947): 4.
38. Demaitre, "She Has a Musical Mission" (caption to photo of Margaret Bonds).

MARGARET BONDS'S SOCIETAL MISSION AND *THE MONTGOMERY VARIATIONS*

The two works that are the subject of this volume, *The Montgomery Variations* and the setting of the W. E. B. Du Bois *Credo*, may be fairly considered the most expansive and concentrated manifestations of several themes that evolved continually over the course of three decades in Margaret Bonds's creative life. They are also pendants to one another. In many ways, they are the summation of a societal project born of these themes that crystallized in the 1960s as the result of Bonds's own personal and professional growth and her rich collaborative friendship with Langston Hughes. The story of this chapter is the story of those themes' emergence and coalescence into the extraordinary artistic identity that is the historic legacy of Margaret Bonds.

Heritage: Sex and Race, Art and Destiny

Estella Bonds's vision in raising Margaret as a fearlessly individualistic artist and woman began to bear fruit early on. As we have seen, it gave Margaret the strength she needed not just to endure and defy the dehumanizing systemic racism of the world around her, earning both her bachelor's and master's degrees at a prestigious university in a field – classical music – that resolutely marginalized Blacks and women. It also gave Margaret, as a seventeen-year-old in her first semester of her sophomore year at Northwestern, the self-confidence needed to give the national premiere of Florence Price's first *Fantasie nègre* at the national meeting of the National Association of Negro Musicians in 1930 and, shortly after the completion of her master's degree, to premiere Price's D-minor Piano Concerto at the Chicago

Figure 1.1 Carl Van Vechten: *Portrait of Margaret Bonds*, October 10, 1956.
Carl Van Vechten Papers Relating to African American Arts and Letters, James
Weldon Johnson Collection in the Yale Collection of American Literature,
Beinecke Rare Book and Manuscript Library, Yale University. ©Van Vechten
Trust.

World's Fair in 1934.[1] And it endowed her with the vision to
continue to pursue that artistic mission after receiving her master's degree, touring regionally with John Greene (1901–60s[2])
and as a soloist, studying with Will Marion Cook (1869–1944)
and William Levi Dawson (1899–1990), building connections on
both sides of the color line in the Chicago arts world, founding
her Allied Arts Academy in Chicago, and eventually, in the
depths of the Great Depression, relocating from Chicago to
Harlem in order to pursue her life's work in the United States'
largest city. Harlem was the adopted home of not only Langston
Hughes but also W. E. B. Du Bois, Countee Cullen, and more
than 450,000 Black Americans, most of whom had moved there
as part of the Great Migration, pursuing for themselves and their
children the hope and dream of a life of freedom and equality that
was systemically denied them in the Jim Crow South.

It was also in New York that Bonds would study with Emerson Harper, Roy Harris (1898–1979), Djane Lavoie-Herz (1888–1982), and Robert Starer (1924–2001), and there that she achieved her early victories in the stylistic cohabitation of music vernacular and cultivated, Black and White, that would become one of the hallmarks of her creative imagination. Bonds's early New York years witnessed the composition of popular songs such as "Georgia" and "Peach Tree Street," spirituals such as the *Creek-Freedmen Spirituals*, and the publication of her visionary setting of Hughes's "The Negro Speaks of Rivers."

And it was in New York, too, that she met and married Lawrence (Larry) Richardson in 1940. Although Bonds would move to California without Richardson in 1967, their *de facto* separation was the result not of marital strife or estrangement, but of Bonds's pursuit of her career and Richardson's support for her in that pursuit. The many surviving letters between the two document the intersection of that pursuit with the composer's pride in her matrilineal and racial heritage and religious faith, and how this intersection gave her with a pronounced sense of destiny and independence.

These elements came to the fore in 1942–3, during a difficult period in the Bonds–Richardson marriage. The United States had entered World War II in December 1941, and the resultant surge in the West Coast economy produced significant opportunities in a range of fields. Because of these circumstances, Margaret Bonds and Larry Richardson, then married just over two years and with no children,[3] agreed that she and her duo-piano partner, Calvin Jackson (1919–85), would go to Los Angeles for eight weeks and try to secure a position in the booming California entertainment industry that would be sufficiently lucrative to enable Richardson to move to California with her.

That position never came, and indeed the long-distance relationship introduced serious strains into the couple's relatively young marriage. Those circumstances produced a rich series of deeply personal and emotional letters that reveal much about the issues that Bonds and Richardson faced, and gave the composer occasion to discuss the challenges she encountered in her work and to explain her attitudes toward these challenges. One of the most important of these letters, hereinafter referred to as her "Destiny letter," was written on December 17, 1942. It is lengthy (twelve pages) and, according to the next letter in the series, was written under the influence of alcohol. The "God be my judge!" that stands boldly written at the top of the first page was apparently written postscriptum. Because of the insights the letter provides into Bonds's ideas and her biography at a crucial stage in her professional development, the letter's text is only lightly abbreviated here:

God be my judge!
Larry, my dear,

Speaking of love, I have loved you with a love you could never find again. The sacrifices I have made for and because of you, you shall never know. I have never told you, nor shall I ever. That is my way – SILENCE. Either you have seen and know, or you haven't seen, and don't know. If you don't see, and don't know I shall never tell you. I will die with the secret.

Coming home tonight and reading your letter was a "fitting climax." We were given a week's notice. This owner was kinder. He gave us a week, whereas the other man gave us one night!

I cannot speak for Calvin. He probably humored Zelda with letters because she is nineteen and a child. As for you, I have been thinking that you were an adult; however, I have been on my guard, for at this moment, I have four letters in my purse to you that are unmailed. They are letters in which I poured out my innards. *Then* I thought they might worry you, and did not mail them. I shall keep them for an auto-biography [*sic*], if I ever achieve the greatness I believe I shall attain.

It is difficult to write letters when one is fighting – fighting. If one has any feelings at all – and I *am* an artist to my finger-tips, and emotional – it is certain that anxiety, fear, and all the other emotions will creep in.

There have been times when I have been walking down the street with Calvin and burst into tears – I've wanted you so much. But you "challenged" me, remember? It would have been easy to send to you for money, or to get on the first train and come home – so easy. It would be so easy for Calvin to take some other jobs without me – for he is ready-fitted for *anything*. But he *loves* me and believes in me and in my music; he believes that together we can crack a field for Negroes that has never been touched – so we suffer together.

When I left, you remember I woke up crying every day. How much easier it would be for me to stay home with you and our dogs. Heavenly moments! I remember a surprise air-raid – we wrapped our arms around each other – ready to die together. Those are the moments of escape. Blondie and Brownie sat on the floor – silently – as though they knew the world might come to an end. I felt safe, because I was in your arms.

Speaking of Blondie and Brownie, this year I tried hard to have a baby. No baby came. I thought it would assure your not going to the Army. I didn't believe you when you said you didn't want a baby. I knew that your emotions were being repressed by your common sense – your practicalness. You think I couldn't be a good mother. I could be! I have all the instincts any other woman has.

But I am conflicted because you "challenge me." If only I could have been left alone – to work out my Destiny as I planned it. I remember 15 W. 123rd[4] the night you stormed out of the house because I didn't want to teach school. Then you found some quotation in the dresser afterward – I can't remember what it was, and you thought I was going to leave you – and you found tobacco on the dresser – it was Maple and Rum; I had bought it for you, and had used a bit with that cigarette maker I had – so for a moment you thought that I had been unfaithful to you. How you have mistrusted me at times.

I didn't hardly know that wives were ever unfaithful to their husbands at that time. I learned it, really, from you – noble one. My own conscience has been so clear – it enabled me to be freer. I began to lie and be secretive lately; New York did that for me. Before then I was the complete extrovert. What a believing fool!

But I am rambling, because I am unhappy and conflicted. My heart tells me to get on the train and come home. My mind tells me "No." My mind tells me that if you honestly love me as I love you, you will allow me to work out my Destiny – this time; that is, that you will leave me "as the lilies of the field" – "they toil not, neither do they spin." Strange things are happening to me from the career standpoint. I feel that I should relax – at least for the eight weeks I have here [–] and let them happen. . . .

The Morris Agency here has done nothing for us. I hated to tell you. I've tried to spare you the anxiety I've had to go through – the desire to win – the feeling that we must not come back "empty-handed," "licked." . . . [Calvin and I are] big spirits, so we forgive but we don't forget, after the way we've shared and sacrificed for this – for our Mothers, you, Zelda, and Paul too – and for the Race! Wonder if we'll get any thanks. Maybe we're not really great and it doesn't count. Maybe your bed and my bed being warm, and Calvin and Zelda being together, and Calvin's mother being evicted – and the money you've lent us is *much* more important. Maybe. Maybe we're just impractical dreamers! So was [*sic*] Marian Anderson, Brahms, Vronsky and Babin, your dear Hazel Scott and Lena and all the rest of them.[5]

My Mother is the only person who has not reproached us. She believes in me – and has known Calvin since he was a baby – hardly able to reach his hands to the keyboard. She has sent me two blouses to wear. She would have sent me money if necessary. She *loves* me. She is willing to die with nothing [so] that I shall fulfill my Destiny. Perhaps, she too, is an impractical dreamer. She wanted me to marry, have children, be a good wife, stay at home with you – but she also knows that the cohabitation of herself and my father did not make *that* combination. She endures and accepts – for she sees – she knows – she knows that as there is the

Sun I shall win. Whether she lives to see it or not is not important to her. All she has ever demanded of me is that I try – married or single. From my grandfather on down [my ancestors] all worked silently, quietly, in obscurity for Mankind, for our oppressed Race. They are not Conventional people. They are individualists – thus their unhappiness and isolation. They are accountable to God, and God takes care of them. My believing in the Forces of Nature – I can't help it. I was born to it. My Optimism? It is rooted in the earth in the tree my grandfather planted – in the mulberry bush Margaret (my aunt planted) [*sic*] [and] in the lilac bush I went out in the yard with Helen to prune every year. The Bonds' – they are considered "fools" – my grandmother, the child once removed from slavery, and my grandfather, the product of slaves and Indians – and my grandmother's father – an Irish imigrant [*sic*] – a man of courage who came over in steerage, and made good – and my own father who has great intellect – and who would have been a great man had he not tried to conform to the taboos, inhibitions and the rest of them – these are my blood, my soul, I cannot help myself; this great desire to win. They all won before me and I must go farther. I can not be compared to women who are called "Baby" by cheap entertainers – or to Una Mae Carlysle [*sic*],[6] or Lena Horne, or Hazel Scott – noone [*sic*] came over in steerage for them, or went through years of med school, or cleared cinders, or went without so they could have a college education. Noone [*sic*] sheltered, and protected, and ate beans so they could be great. – if anyone ate beans it was because they had to – not because they wanted to. . . .[7]

The takeaways from this letter are many and complicated. For one thing, it reveals the importance of a sense of solidarity and support to Margaret Bonds's creative life, a sense of community and helping hands that is also manifest in her education and career generally in the pronounced sense of sisterhood she enjoyed with the other members of Alpha Kappa Alpha.[8] This pronounced need for solidarity correlates meaningfully with the importance of collaborations in Bonds's creative life.

More important, however, is that this letter shows how Margaret Bonds's musical "mission" (as it would be described in a 1964 *Washington Post* interview[9]) was inextricably bound up with her general *Destiny* (upper-case *D*), and how Bonds considered this *Destiny* itself to be a sort of ancestral charge – one that placed upon her shoulders a personal and professional imperative to use her music to address and right the societal ills that had forced her mother, her father, and her grandparents and great-grandparents to work "silently, quietly, in obscurity for Mankind, for our oppressed Race."

"A Responsibility to Her Heritage"

Margaret Bonds would return to New York and Larry Richardson in 1943, but she was far from "licked" – indeed, if anything, the difficulty of that stay in Los Angeles seems to have strengthened her conviction that this ancestral charge to "go farther" was a God-given opportunity to artists. Her work and her letters of the coming years bespeak a sense of responsibility to create and promulgate a Black American identity in art that – in the context of a society that persisted in dehumanizing Blackness – evinced pride in the Black condition and Black experience, that was cognizant of what Bonds termed "a responsibility to [Black] heritage" and authentic to the modern Black experience. This theme is hardly surprising, of course – but in the profoundly segregated world of concert music in the United States during Bonds's lifetime (and today),[10] it posed a significant challenge that Bonds and all Black Americans had to continually negotiate and renegotiate with their every creative utterance if they did not want their art to remain marginalized, underfunded, and systematically written out of narratives of music's history such as the ones Bonds experienced in her own collegiate career. The pervasive systemic racism of the world of concert music marginalized music and musicians of color on the stages, minimized Black Americans' access to and enfranchisement in concerts, suppressed Black creativity that did not conform to (and thus affirm) White expectations of Black creativity based on racist stereotypes, and essentially made it necessary for Black musicians to organize and maintain their own cultural institutions that would provide a home for Black classical creativity – orchestras, opera companies, and organizations such as the National Association of Negro Musicians.

Bonds's earliest surviving epistolary comment on this complex set of issues is found in a letter to Hughes dated May 8, 1937. She had just attended a theater production in Evanston and taken the long commute back to her home on the south side of segregated Chicago. Despite the late hour, she took the time to type a note to her recent friend: "Its [*sic*] three o'clock in the morning. I just returned from Evanston where I saw a lousy Negro play written by

a white man – a very nice white man too, but he doesn't know how to write a Negro play."[11]
The "Negro play" in question was Albert R. Crews's (1908–59) *Let My People Go*, written for Crews's master's thesis and performed under his own direction in Northwestern's University Theatre on April 5–7, 1937,[12] and the difficulties it encountered clarify what Bonds meant when she said that Crews "[didn't] know how to write a Negro play." Its subject was "Negro relationships in modern society," and in the course of the play the protagonist, in "scholastic surroundings," experiences "difficulties in coming to grips with a world unprepared to recognize his abilities";[13] its "ill-fated" heroine was "an exotic," and "as such" "above race."[14] It also included "a close relationship between a white girl and a negro boy" that was modified in performance because "this whole situation struck [Crews] as possibly not acceptable to the average theatre-goer."[15] It began as a play "concerned with racial problems" and concluded as "a denouncement of corrupt politics."[16] In an article published in the *Daily Northwestern* on the day of the premiere, the playwright noted that "[t]here are many unpleasant things that come up whenever you deal with the race question. . . . The resulting reaction on a cast half negro, half white has not been easy on them."[17] Additionally, the playwright/director had difficulty finding enough Black players to participate in the play's racially mixed cast: on April 13, after rehearsals had begun, the *Daily Northwestern* reported that a sign had been placed above the door of the university's School of Speech reading: "Help wanted: one torch singer, Negro, female; three gangsters, Negro male."[18] The paper also reported that the "controversial" play's "vigorous climaxes" contained several fight scenes that resulted in one broken nose during rehearsals.

These factors make it easy enough to understand Bonds's description of *Let My People Go* as "lousy" because the playwright "[didn't] know how to write a Negro play." Most obviously, the play cultivates racial stereotypes – exotic seductress singers, brawling Black gangster men, Blacks as fundamentally out of place in academic environments – that certainly would have been irksome for Bonds as a modern middle-class Black woman who, by this point, had earned both her bachelor's and master's degrees in classical music from a prestigious university. More, the press accounts suggest that the play contained no hint of the deeply religious community life of the Black church, which for Bonds and many other Blacks was a defining aspect of the Black American experience.[19] Nor did it reflect any ethos of uplift or edification: Black women were seductive singers; Black men were by nature violent and out of place in scholastics; and Black life was generally hopeless, dreadful. The Black experience depicted in Crews's play offered no source of pride, no hope, nothing authentic to Bonds's own outlook.

The element of pride in the dignity, humanity, and fundamental beauty of Blackness so noticeably lacking in Crews's play is, as we shall see, central to Margaret Bonds's *Montgomery Variations* and *Credo* – and it is something that Bonds wrote of with touching eloquence two decades later, in March of 1961. While in Nassau for a performance of *The Ballad of the Brown King*, she penned a letter to Langston Hughes that describes some of the things that, for her, constituted the authentic Black experience:

I think of you frequently as I walk along the streets here, or wherever I am – for you play such an important part in God's scheme of things. Yesterday I bought you the brown policeman doll – for I am so impressed with the tall, brown-black men who control so many items here.

Yesterday a little dark-brown-skin-girl [*sic*] looked us straight in the face, and with *pride*. Blacks don't "shuffle" here – nor "cringe". They walk, drive their cars, and "walk straight and proud" as though they *really know* that God loves them *intensely*. (The British *can't* be as bad as they've been painted.) Before I left N.Y. I phoned my psychic. I said, "Is it *really* alright for me to go on this trip?["] She said, "Yes, you will have a great spiritual experience." I am having it in more ways than one. If you are home, please call my Baby Djane to tell her "hello." One day I will bring her to this wondrous place – God be willing.[20]

This letter offers a stark contrast to Crews's perhaps well-meant but ultimately cheap and demeaning perspective on the Black condition that Bonds dubbed "lousy" in 1937, as well as rich insights into the vision for Black art that would characterize Bonds's output for most of her career, including *The Montgomery Variations* and *Credo*. To begin with, the letter veritably exudes the deep religiosity and spirituality so conspicuously lacking in the play. Moreover, although the letter is most obviously a description of the lives of Blacks in the Bahamas (still a British colony when it was penned), it is also, by way of comparison, a critical commentary on the prejudices, limitations, and demeaning attitudes that Bonds and other Black folk faced every day in the United States.

Also revealing, though, is Bonds's statement that Hughes "play[ed] such an important part in God's scheme of things," for this observation reflects Bonds's lifelong and increasingly prominent conviction that racial equality and sincere belief in the inherent dignity and humanity of Blackness were of God, that she and all people had a significant role to play in a "scheme of things" that would bring about that divinely mandated condition of racial pride and global equality. To turn one's back on this role would be to abet the deferment of the dream;[21] to embrace it, to embrace God's divine will.

Bonds's belief in that divine mission and in the imperative for Black racial pride also had another dimension, one that intersects with her sense of Destiny and history's imperative that she, as an African American woman, "go farther." A summary of this other dimension was occasioned by soprano Adele Addison's (b. 1925) second recital in New York's Town Hall (December 15, 1963). Addison's adventurous program included music by Barber, Dallapicolla, Duparc, Schubert, and Wolf. It was positively reviewed by influential critic Harold C. Schonberg, but Margaret Bonds expressed a different view in a letter to Hughes written two days later:

God bless Betty [Allen] for taking us all out of the "ghetto" – and not one of us will be completely out of it until *all* American singers start thinking this way.

[Adele] Addison defied criticism Sunday night, but not a "brother" listed on the program. Nevertheless she's truly great now, and she is maturing, so perhaps one day she'll get the "message" and realize that she has a responsibility to her heritage as a "club member." Her audience Sunday night was mostly people of color.[22]

This letter is a comparison of the programming choices of legendary mezzo-soprano Betty Allen (1927–2009) and those of Addison. Allen (who had made her own Town Hall debut in 1958, and who was described by Raoul Abdul as having "a voice

27

with the richness and vibrancy of a fine cello"[23]) frequently programmed music by Black American composers, including Bonds, and had recently sent Bonds two programs from her recitals in Germany, recitals that included some of Bonds's settings of Hughes's poems. While Bonds applauds Addison's brilliance and courage in commingling canonical music with more daring works such as Dallapiccola's *Quattro liriche di Antonio Machado*, she was disappointed that Addison, singing for an audience that was "mostly people of color," sang no music by composers of color and effectively denied those composers a place on the concert stage. Moreover, Addison's programming missed a valuable opportunity to share with her Black audience members any music by composers whose lives and music resonated with their own lived experiences and lived sufferings. In so doing, she deferred the dream of a musical experience that would be open and inclusive, celebratory of Black artistry – and this was tantamount to ducking her "responsibility to her heritage as a 'club member.'"

Bonds's outlook is astonishing in its beauty and courage. Her education and career had taught her well that the world worked vociferously to dehumanize Black folk, to subjugate and denigrate them, make them an out-group. But for her, being Black made one a "club member," a member of an *in-group* that had the privilege of a rich and distinguished inheritance and thus a responsibility to cultivate and celebrate that heritage for the world to see. W. E. B. Du Bois's words in a crucial article of his *Credo* aptly distill this outlook: "Especially do I believe in the Negro Race; in the beauty of its genius, the sweetness of its soul, and its strength in that meekness which shall yet inherit this turbulent earth."

Coalescence

Margaret Bonds's correspondence leading up to the decade that produced *The Montgomery Variations* and the *Credo* reveals the themes in her personality and creative outlook that, as we shall see, ultimately coalesced into those poetic utterances: the belief in personal Destiny; a celebration of the inherent beauty and dignity of the Black condition; a sense that that condition, like personal Destiny itself, was God-given and thus holy; and a conviction that artists, musical and other, were to use their art to celebrate and further these things as a cause. These themes manifested themselves with increasing brilliance and boldness as her creative collaboration with Hughes deepened into a new journey that spanned the remaining years of their friendship in the 1960s and continued beyond Hughes's death in 1967.

Like most journeys, this one had stations – points of arrival and departure that articulated the composer's progress toward her goal. The first of these stopping points occurred almost by accident, for Bonds's *Shakespeare in Harlem* is incidental music to a play created from a collection of poems that had been published seventeen years earlier. The original collection of "light verse" (Hughes's description),[24] its title derived from a short and saucy poem of the same name, is significant partly as the fourth published collection of poems by the popularly anointed "poet laureate of the Negro race" and partly because of its creative synthesis of poetry, visual art, and music. Cast as seven sets of vignettes centered on the Black experience in Harlem, the collection returns Hughes to the experimental blues poetry that had made his fame in the 1920s, synthesizing this with the social activism that had characterized much of his work in the 1930s.[25] Initial critical response was mixed, with Owen Dodson of Clark Atlanta University decrying the collection as "lazy, unpoetic, common and vulgar" and the *Negro History Bulletin* naming it Book of the Month on its "Children's Page": "[the] poems are apparently in a humorous vein, but at the same time they show the deepest thought as to the serious condition of the Negro. ... To [Hughes] all the world is sad and dreary everywhere he roams, but still he can laugh in the hope for a brighter day."[26]

But the collection *Shakespeare in Harlem* is also important for the social significance of its structure, which immediately proclaims the multifaceted Black experience, represented by blues, dice rolling, prostitution, a charismatic preacher, a young gang member, a girl in a bar, and a Black college student in White-dominated academia as coequal to, or perhaps latter-day envoicings of, the same ideas, ideals, loves, and beauties given poetic expression by the iconic Renaissance bard. Harlem dialogue, scenes, and characters are intermingled with witty and often brilliant allusions to other vernacular "high" literature, rendering meaningless the accepted boundaries between "high" (cultivated, canonical, and White) and "low" (folk, noncanonical, and Black) literature, life, and art.

By the late 1950s, the volume and its socially and culturally symbolic title had become so well known that White playwright Robert Glenn (fl. 1940–60) sought and received Hughes's permission to combine excerpts into a one-act play that would dramatize the poetry of the Black experience. An initial run in Westport, Connecticut, in August, 1959, was sufficiently successful to occasion a one-night performance at the Theatre de Lys in Greenwich Village on October 27, 1959; Hughes recommended that Bonds compose music for the play. By December 4, 1959, she was reporting her discussions of the project with the playwright back to Hughes,[27] and the play opened off-Broadway on February 10, 1960, with Bonds's score included. That score, lamentably, is still unpublished, but *New York Times* reviewer Brooks Atkinson described it as "subdued but stirring."[28] The poems' (and the play's) commingling of disparate styles and idioms was perfectly suited to Bonds's own style; the work's social mission of cultivating Black American cultural pride by celebrating the Black experience in authentic poetry and music on stage still more so. After the performance at the Theatre de Lys, Hughes wrote candidly about the contribution Bonds's score made to the effect of the whole: "Your part in that 'Shakespeare in Harlem' was most effective. I was more conscious of the dramatic value of the music at the de Lys than I was in Westport. It came in so naturally – and just right."[29]

The second station in the journey that led Bonds to *The Montgomery Variations* and *Credo* likewise had earlier roots: the collaborative cantata *The Ballad of the Brown King*, a Christmas cantata whose title derives from the eleventh-century description of one of the magi, Balthazar, by Pseudo-Bede (Manegold von Lautenbach, ca. 1030–ca. 1103), as being "a dark, fully bearded king."[30] This description rebuts White portrayals of the magi as White, thus countermanding White culture's erasure of significant Blacks from history. More importantly, it reinstates Black folk into the central narrative of Black Christianity, recognizes a Black magus, and – especially significant in the context of the systemic racism of the United States – portrays the wise Balthazar as an equal of the other wise men who celebrated the arrival of the newborn Christ the King.

The Ballad of the Brown King was first composed in 1954 and premiered in New York in December of that year, in a version that consisted of seven movements and was scored for soloists, chorus, and piano.[31] By December 27, 1955, Bonds wrote to Hughes that she was hard at work orchestrating the work, but poet and composer then undertook significant revisions, discarding one movement of the original and adding three new ones. By August 24, 1960, Bonds had finished the orchestration of the revised version,[32] and that version was premiered on December 11, 1960, in Clark Auditorium at the YWCA on 50th Street at 8th Avenue in New York. The performance was a great success, and by May 3, 1961, Sam Fox Publishing Company, one of the largest music publishers in the United States, had sent three copies of a contract to Langston Hughes for his and Margaret Bonds's signatures.[33] More performances of the piano–vocal version followed in 1961, and on December 26 of that year Margaret Bonds's own orchestration (which at this writing is out of print) was premiered under the baton of Irving Bunton (1933–2016) on a nationally broadcast CBS television special titled *Christmas U.S.A.*

The Ballad of the Brown King was an immediate hit, receiving dozens of performances across the United States within its first year and enjoying wide popularity for the rest of Bonds's life. Several times plans for a recording were laid, and it was performed as far away as Nigeria. The reasons for its appeal are obvious – the landmark *Brown v. Board of Education* decision and the Montgomery bus boycott had launched the mature Civil Rights Movement, and major initiatives for bolstering the legal standing of African Americans were unfolding with almost every passing week. The subject of the work and Hughes's delicate and unpretentious verse affirming the equal participation of a Black magus in a festival celebrated globally resonated broadly and deeply. More, Margaret Bonds's music was not only beautiful but also extraordinary in a broader historical sense: it is at first blush a classical cantata for soprano and baritone soloists with mixed chorus and piano (or orchestra), but Bonds's music virtuosically blends the idioms of classical, calypso, gospel, and jazz to an unprecedented extent. In *The Ballad of the Brown King*, the project of breaking down the artistic and social barriers that segregated Black composers, Black poets, and the Black experience generally from what Ashley Jackson has aptly termed "the predominantly-white, elite American musical establishment" took a significant step forward – and struck a chord that resonated with its time.

With *The Ballad of the Brown King* behind her, Margaret Bonds took another step forward in the musical and societal project that would result in *The Montgomery Variations*. The next step was the Easter cantata *Simon Bore the Cross*. A liturgical complement and conceptual pendant to *The Ballad of the Brown King*, *Simon Bore the Cross* was the story of Simon of Cyrene, the Black man who was chosen by the Romans to bear the cross of Jesus of Nazareth on the Via Dolorosa. By the early twentieth century, Simon had come to signify Blackness in theater and poetry, as in the 1924 poem "Simon the Cyrenian Speaks" by Countee Cullen, the great Harlem Renaissance poet who was himself a friend of Hughes and Bonds.[34] In that poem, which may have been an immediate source of inspiration for Bonds's cantata, Simon at first resists taking the cross, saying that he had been chosen only "because my skin is black," but then changes his mind:

> It was Himself my pity bought;
> I did for Christ alone
> What all of Rome could not have wrought
> With bruise of lash or stone.[35]

Bonds approached Hughes with the idea for this collaboration sometime in the late summer or early autumn of 1962, and by September 26 she was able to report to Hughes that Ralph Satz of Sam Fox Music (the publisher of *The Ballad of the Brown King*) was eager to take this project under his wing also.[36]

Like *The Ballad of the Brown King*, *Simon Bore the Cross* corrects White culture's erasure of Blacks' participation in historically significant events and foregrounds the vital contribution of a Black man to one of the holiest series of events of the Christian liturgical year; and like the *Ballad*, *Simon* integrates this religiously and socially symbolic source of Black cultural pride into a cantata that, by genre, was traditionally the province of the White-dominated cultural spheres that were the agents of that very historical erasure.[37] In Hughes's libretto, Mary watches with wonder and marvels at Simon's compassion and dark beauty: "Who is that man who goes to help my son? ... Who shares the suffering of my Jesus, the glory of my precious son? ... So dark, so beautiful his face. Look at this face so strong and full of grace." And, perhaps most importantly, this "strong" and "beautiful" African shares in the burden of the suffering Christ bore for humanity's salvation, and does so with strength and dignity: "Black men will share the pain of the cross, black men will share the pain" (No. 5); "Jesus and Simon, brothers together, they walked, and the African was strong, trudging on in the dust of humanity's disgrace" (No. 6); "Now the king of the Jews had to die, death was his glory. The Cyrenian bore the cross, the African bore the cross, the cross to save our souls, the cross for you and me" (No. 6).

But with *Simon*, Margaret Bonds takes a significant further step in the project of boldly transgressive erasure of the barriers to cultural and societal integration. The plot of *Simon* reduplicates almost exactly that of one of the most revered masterpieces of White European music, the *Matthäus-Passion* of J. S. Bach; and *Simon*'s stylistic melding of seemingly incongruous musical styles is comparable to that of *The Ballad of the Brown King*. What is more, *Simon Bore the Cross* is a cantus firmus cantata after the model of Bach's chorale cantatas – but its cantus firmus is not a (White) chorale or hymn, but rather the African American spiritual "And He Never Said a Mumblin' Word" (also known as *Crucifixion*). A prefatory note dated January 31, 1965, in the autograph score shows that Bonds was well aware of the significance of this gesture:

After the success of the Christmas Cantata "The Ballad of the Brown King" Ralph Satz, editor at Sam Fox[,] requested that I compose another cantata based on the Negro Spiritual "He Never Said a Mumblin' Word." I invited Langston Hughes to write a text and to fashion a story around the African who bore Jesus' Cross.

Both Mr. Hughes and I have more work to do on this cantata, I am well aware. As it now stands, however, it may be the only work of its kind, for to my knowledge, noone [sic] before now has based a cantata on a Negro Spiritual theme.[38]

Creating *The Montgomery Variations*

Although Bonds's prefatory note to the final score of *Simon Bore the Cross* shows her awareness of the work's historical significance, the cantata was also significant in her personal growth. For with the provisional completion of *Simon Bore the Cross* ca. 1963, Margaret Bonds had composed a large-scale cyclical composition that celebrated Black folk and portrayed Black suffering as the historical antecedent to the redemption of "humanity's disgrace" and its salvation through God's divine will – one, moreover, in which all movements were based on the same theme; one whose musical genre and central styles the White-dominated musical establishment broadly apathetic or inimical to Black spirituals and the cause of racial justice considered its own. But Bonds subverts that White dominance even as she employs it in the service of her own musical and societal project. *Simon Bore the Cross* reveals Margaret Bonds to be a composer who was compositionally ready to undertake the project that would become *The Montgomery Variations*: a seven-movement programmatic symphonic variation cycle that was based on the spiritual "I Want Jesus to Walk with Me" and affirmed the dignity and humanity of the Black experience by celebrating the courage, nobility, and faith of Blacks. But *The Montgomery Variations* celebrates not historical and biblical Black folk, but rather the living and breathing contemporary Blacks whose courage and resolve were the motivators and engines of the Civil Rights Movement.

There is a kind of poetry to what happened next, for in the first nine months of 1964 the energy that Bonds and Hughes had been pouring into *Simon Bore the Cross* yielded to circumstances born of the two artists' busy schedules and prolificness, and to the daily unfolding momentous events in the Civil Rights Movement: it is as if that inspiration and creative momentum dispersed itself into Bonds's and Hughes's respective and separate activities in the second half of 1963, delaying any further mention of the cantata for a full fifteen months. As Allegra Martin has shown,[39] Bonds and Hughes were working enthusiastically on *Simon* in the early spring of 1963, but Hughes's trips abroad and Bonds's tour as accompanist for the Melodaires, a six-voice male choir of Black singers, interrupted the process. That tour was significant, for it took Bonds deep into the tense and dangerous Jim Crow South. It was not her first trip to the South (she had traveled there on concert tours as early as 1938) but on this trip, too, Bonds she experienced firsthand the lived sufferings, the lived courage, and Southern Blacks' lived commitment to the cause of racial justice.

It made a deep and lasting impression, as did another Southern tour that Bonds and the Melodaires undertook the following year. As we will see in Chapter 2, the 1963 tour inspired the first six movements of *The Montgomery Variations* – and in the summer of 1964 Bonds wrote the concluding (seventh) movement. That process was not lacking in poetry of its own. In writing the first six movements, she adapted an unpublished orchestral score from June 1959 titled "Variations in D Minor" under the new title "Dawn in Dixie"[40] – so that the compositional beginning of her new contribution to the freedom movement was what she described as an "awaken[ing]" "to the fact that something new was happening in the South" (see Chapter 2, p. 50), and the last movement, penned as that atmosphere of hope spread with the passage of a landmark Civil Rights Act and much more, became the radiantly beautiful "Benediction" that closed the *Variations*.

By September 6, 1964, Bonds was able to report that she had played the completed *Montgomery Variations* for baritone Raoul Abdul, who had been Langston Hughes's personal assistant since 1958. This long and emotional letter, occasioned mostly by Bonds's frustrations with Abdul, confirms that Bonds, at the piano, had played through *The Montgomery Variations* for Abdul, to his approval:

Dear Raoul said one day on the phone "*I* can't figure you out." Why should he at his stage of development try to figure *me* out. It would take all his time to figure himself out. . . . He should "go sing" or "go write" – or whatever it is he wants to do. Right now I'm still "bugged" by Raoul. . . . After eating my food "cooked with LOVE" – listening to my Montgomery Variations written with love, devotion to the Negro Race and Humanity, and God and everything noble, in discussing a dress I am making he suggested that I was trying to "out-do" Hortense Love.[41]

My motivation for doing *anything* never could be to "out-do" anyone. This is just *not* a part of my personality. I am aware that some *have* to compete to do, but I never *do*. My credo goes something in this fashion: "Lord, I'm not anything without you; you gave me this talent, and I know you meant me to develope [*sic*] it and share it with anyone who wants it. Guide me in using it to the best of my ability. I know I am accountable only to *You* [for] what I do with it, Lord," – and then I might go on – "I'm not certain the majority of your children will ever understand what I'm about, but as long as I half-way please you I can stay psychiatrically happy."

Now, I kind of think this is very much your Credo, too . . .
Now, as I've said before, I'm sure Raoul *means* well. However, he tells different tales all the time. Maybe its [*sic*] because he sees both sides of a question. (Laugh!)

For instance, one time you, Langston[,] are so great you should write with Leonard Bernstein or M[orton] Gould. Now, on this last visit *my* music is so dramatic I, Margaret (quote Raoul)[,] should have done *Tambourines*.[42]
He gleefully prefaced this with "I don't think Mr. Hughes is going to write words to your music, Margaret."
Listening to my "Montgomery Variations" he was all praise – and "you're so dramatic!" He mentioned a "brother" – and I wasn't sure whether he wanted me to do orchestrations for his "brother's" score or a score for you, or what he wanted – or maybe he wants me to be subservient – as all women should be, and come crawling and begging you for a book.[43]

The handwriting in this lengthy and deeply conflicted letter shows that it was written in haste, not composed – and this bespeaks the openness, spontaneity, and candor that the relationship between Bonds and Hughes had attained after nearly thirty years of friendship and collaboration. Directly relevant here, though, are Bonds's description of *The Montgomery Variations* as a work "written with love, devotion to the Negro Race and Humanity, and God and everything noble" (an apt description, as we shall see in Chapter 2), and her demonstration that the work stood completed already before September 6, 1964 (the letter does not specify the exact date when she played it for Abdul). At some point, possibly around this same time, she also wrote a program that detailed the extramusical ideas and events that the work's seven movements describe (see Chapter 2).

The subsequent fate of *The Montgomery Variations* is distressingly similar to that of most of Bonds's works. She set it aside in 1965–66 to work on her setting of the *Credo* of W. E. B. Du Bois – an even more ambitious musical civil-rights project. Virtually every passing week of those years, populated as they were with the increasing urgency of the Civil Rights Movement and news of the increasing casualties in the undeclared war in Vietnam, brought events both domestic and international that only increased the two works' relevance for contemporary performers and audiences. And so, in mid-1966, Bonds turned to the significant task of bringing them to the broader public in performance.

One of her first steps in this project was to solicit the opinion and advocacy of her friend and former student Ned Rorem (1923–2022), to whom she apparently had mentioned the work previously.[44] On June 21, 1966, she wrote: "Here is 'The Montgomery Variations.' I wrote a rather elaborate program for it – but then decided perhaps the explanation might hurt the piece rather than help it."[45] Rorem replied on July 4 with a letter that may puzzle those who know the score:

Dearest Margaret –

Thanks for your very good letter which I should have answered ages ago, but I've been all over the map since then . . .

Thanks also for your score which I've looked at with careful interest. I shall be frank. The theme is good (is it yours, or a Spiritual?). However, the *variety* implied in a title like VARIATIONS is – for me – lacking. There's not one key change, and hardly even an accidental, for the first 48 pages, and then you merely modulate to the major. Your idea was of course to make a suite on one tonality, as Bach did, but Bach used very different material in each movement, while you employ not only the same thematic material in each section, but you hardly alter it beyond the devices of diminution and augmentation. I do love the feeling of nostalgia, especially in the slower movements; I'm less convinced of the rhythmic sections (too square). My impression is that the whole thing should be "shrunk" into a one-movement rhapsody. Perhaps the best thing (I mean the most *successful* thing) is the orchestration which looks shimmering and foolproof – although you might want to simplify the harp part here & there.

You're right not to include program notes: the titles are sufficient. . . . What should I do now? I'd be glad to write a note to Bernstein – or whoever – if you wish.

I'm glad you weren't too appaled [*sic*] by the book![46]

As will be shown in Chapter 2, several points of Rorem's critique are ill founded – and Bonds clearly felt the same. She replied with a mixture of gratitude and frank annoyance three days later:

Beloved Ned,

Of course I wasn't appalled by your book – I am promoting it by making little comment about it. . . .

About my score: I admire your frank evaluation. However, I'm certain that I handled this traditional Negro Spiritual theme only to the extent that it should be "handled." The theme is:
"I Want Jesus to Walk with Me"
Do write the note to Bernstein, and when he does it (I'm being positive) won't I love boasting about "how noone [*sic*] would do this score and Ned sent it to Bernstein." (It isn't quite true.) It will be an hour of triumph from many aspects. . . .
P.S. You know I took every word seriously. Perhaps the piece should be titled "Concerning Montgomery" or just "Montgomery" (a set of variations on the spiritual "I Want Jesus to Walk with Me.")
What think you?[47]

Bonds would eventually change her mind about withholding the "elaborate program" and would include that text in a program note for a planned concert that was to include the *Variations* and *The Ballad of the Brown King*. There is no evidence that such a performance actually occurred, but at some point either Rorem or someone else also sent a copy of the program note to Leonard Bernstein.[48] The score for *The Montgomery Variations* is undated, but sometime in 1967 Bonds undertook the significant labor of copying out the parts for what was to be the only performance given during her lifetime. That performance, which paired the *Variations* with Bonds's setting of the Du Bois *Credo* under the baton of her friend Albert McNeil, was given in San Francisco sometime in 1967.[49]

***

The 1967 San Francisco performance is the only documented complete professional performance of *The Montgomery Variations* during Margaret Bonds's lifetime. In December 2018, the University of Connecticut Symphony Orchestra performed the work under the direction of Paul McShee, and three movements were performed by the Nashville Symphony Orchestra in January 2020.[50] The work was finally published by Hildegard Publishing Company (Worcester, MA) in August 2020, and this edition was used for a performance of four movements by the Los Angeles Philharmonic under the baton of Gustavo Dudamel in July 2021.[51]

The half-century of silence that separated the 1967 performance of *The Montgomery Variations* from the work's modern revival is regrettable. So is the work's continued obscurity outside the United States and so is the appearance, in most concerts by major orchestras, of Bonds's music only in excerpt within programs that present canonical works by (mostly) White men in their entirety. Still, there are encouraging signs. In fact, the year 2021 saw one performance of *The Montgomery Variations* every nineteen days, on average. In October of that year the Minnesota Orchestra, under the baton of Scott Yoo, performed *The Montgomery Variations* in its entirety in an open-access streaming program; and since then the work has been taken up also – albeit unfortunately only in excerpt – by leading orchestras, including the Los Angeles Philharmonic (repeated performances), the New York Philharmonic (January 15, 2022, conducted by Thomas Wilkins), the Philadelphia Orchestra (January 16, 2023, conducted by Yannick Nézet-Séguin), and the Boston Symphony Orchestra (March 9–11, 2023, conducted by Thomas Wilkins). Numerous smaller orchestras have programmed the work in its entirety, introducing the music and its program to audiences beyond the reach of the major metropolitan centers. Most importantly, it has been taken up (in complete rather than excerpted form, happily) by college and university ensembles – ensuring that young musicians of the early twenty-first century will see their musical landscape as one that includes rather than excludes Margaret Bonds and increasing the likelihood that they will share that same perspective with their own future students and audiences.

In any event, McNeil's 1967 decision to pair *The Montgomery Variations* with Bonds's setting of the W. E. B. Du Bois *Credo* was a stroke of genius, for those two compositions, taken together, are the cumulative expression of Margaret Bonds's growth over the course of her career. They reflect what must have been her conscious decision to use her art to express the themes and ideas that drove her: fierce pride in the maternal and racial heritage, a deep syncretism of modes of traditionally segregated artistic expression cultivated and vernacular, Black and White; affirmative, hopeful, and *authentic* artistic expression of Black experience; and an abiding belief that the causes of racial justice and global equality were not just morally right but also divinely ordained. Bonds ascribed "love, devotion to the Negro Race and Humanity, and God and everything noble" to *The Montgomery Variations* in

1964, and in 1966 she would declare the "universal Truth"[52] of the *Credo*. Because of those attributes, these two masterpieces stand as Margaret Bonds's summative musical declarations of the ethos of the New Negro movement and the ongoing imperative for global equality.

Notes

1. This concert is one of the most-discussed events in Florence Price's musical life and in the intersection of the two composers' careers. See, for example, Rae Linda Brown, "Selected Orchestral Music of Florence B. Price (1888–1953) in the Context of Her Life and Work" (PhD diss., Yale University, 1987), 128–68; Rae Linda Brown, "Florence B. Price and Margaret Bonds: The Chicago Years," *Black Music Research Bulletin* 12, no. 2 (1990): 11–14 at 13; Rae Linda Brown, "The Woman's Symphony Orchestra of Chicago and Florence B. Price's Piano Concerto in One Movement," *American Music* 11 (1993): 185–205; Rae Linda Brown, "Lifting the Veil: The Symphonies of Florence B. Price" in *Florence Price: Symphonies Nos. 1 and 3*, ed. Rae Linda Brown and Wayne Shirley, Recent Researches in American Music, No. 66 (Middleton, WI: A-R Editions, 2008), xxviii–xxix; Rae Linda Brown, *The Heart of a Woman: The Life and Music of Florence B. Price*, ed. Guthrie B. Ramsey, Jr. (Urbana: University of Illinois Press, 2020), 245–59; Samantha Hannah Oboakorevue Ege, "The Aesthetics of Florence Price: Negotiating the Dissonances of a New World Nationalism" (PhD diss., University of York, 2020), 142–43; Helen Walker-Hill, "Margaret Bonds" in her *From Spirituals to Symphonies: African-American Women Composers and Their Music* (Urbana: University of Illinois Press, 2007), 148.

2. See Darryl Glenn Nettles, *African American Concert Singers before 1950* (Jefferson, NC: McFarland, 2003), 68.

3. Djane Bonds Richardson (d. 2011) was born four years later, in 1946.

4. Bonds's and Richardson's first apartment in New York was 15 W. 123rd Street.

5. Marian Anderson, African American contralto (1897–1993); Johannes Brahms, German composer (1833–97); Vitya Vronsky (1909–92) and Victor Babin (1908–72), famed Russian duo-piano team; Trinidad-born pianist, singer, and actor Hazel Scott (1920–81); actor, dancer, singer, and activist Lena Horne (1917–2010).

6. Jazz singer, pianist, and songwriter Una Mae Carlisle (1915–56).

7. Margaret Bonds (Los Angeles) to Larry Richardson (New York), December 17, 1942 (Georgetown University Bonds Papers, shelfmark GTM-130530, Box 2, folder 3).

8. Bonds joined the historically Black intercollegiate sorority Alpha Kappa Alpha while an undergraduate at Northwestern, and from then until her final years her letters, concert programs, and press reports make clear that her "sorors" were an important source of inspiration, solidarity, and support for her.

9. Christina Demaitre, "She Has a Musical Mission: Developing Racial Harmony; Heritage Motivates Composing Career," *The Washington Post* 87, no. 253 (August 14, 1964): C2.

10. See discussion in the Epilogue, pp. 150–52.

11. Yale JWJ 26, Box 16, folder 370: no 20.

12. The following information about the play is based on materials kindly shared by Charla Burlenda Wilson, Archivist for the Black Experience, Northwestern University.

13. *The Daily Northwestern* (May 5, 1937): 2.

14. *The Daily Northwestern* (May 6, 1937): 1.

15. Albert Crews, "'Let My People Go' Lets Its Dramatist Go," *The Daily Northwestern* (May 5, 1937): 5.

16. Charles Nelson, "Critic Praises Negroes' Work in Theatre Play," *The Daily Northwestern* (May 6, 1937): 1.

17. Crews, "'Let My People Go' Lets Its Dramatist Go," 5.

18. "Help! School of Speech Wants All Available Negroes," *Northwestern Daily* (April 13, 1937): 2.

19. See Henry Louis Gates, Jr., *The Black Church: This Is Our Story, This Is Our Song* (New York: Penguin, 2021); further, Milton C. Sernett (ed.), *African American Religious History: A Documentary Witness* (Durham, NC: Duke University Press, 1999); Timothy E. Fulop and Albert J. Raboteau (eds.), *African-American Religion: Interpretive Essays in History and Culture* (New York: Routledge, 1997); and Robert Joseph Taylor, Linda M. Chatters, and Jeff Levin (eds.), *Religion in the Lives of African Americans: Social, Psychological, and Health Perspectives* (Thousand Oaks, CA: Sage Publications, 2004).

20. Bonds (Nassau) to Hughes (New York), March 23, 1961 (Yale JWJ 26, Box 16, folder 375: no. 258).

21. See Hughes's poem "Harlem," also known as "A Dream Deferred" (1951).

22. Bonds (NYC) to Hughes (NYC), December 17, 1963 (Yale JWJ 16: 26, folder 379, no. 436).

23. Raoul Abdul, *Blacks in Classical Music: A Personal History* (New York: Dodd, Mead & Co., 1977), 99.

24. Langston Hughes, *Shakespeare in Harlem* (New York: Alfred A. Knopf, 1942), Foreword (n.p.).
25. Timo Müller, "The Vernacular Sonnet and the Afro-Modernist Project," in his *The African American Sonnet: A Literary History* (Jackson: University Press of Mississippi, 2018), 75–90, at 77.
26. Owen Dodson, "*Shakespeare in Harlem*," *Phylon (1940–1956)* 3 (1942): 137–38; "Book of the Month," *Negro History Bulletin* 5 (1942): 157.
27. Bonds (New York) to Hughes (New York), Yale JWJ 26, Box 16, folder 372: no. 123.
28. Brooks Atkinson, "Theatre: 'Shakespeare in Harlem': Langston Hughes Show Opens at 41st Street 'God's Trombones' Seen on Same Program," *New York Times* (February 10, 1950): 43.
29. Letter from Hughes to Bonds, October 30, 1959 (Manuscripts, Archives and Rare Books Division, Schomburg Center for Research in Black Culture, The New York Public Library, Margaret Bonds Papers shelfmark MG873, Box 6, folder 2).
30. Bruce K. Waltke and James M. Houston, with Erika Moore, *The Psalms as Christian Worship: A Historical Commentary* (Grand Rapids, MI: William B. Eerdmans, 2010), 189.
31. On *The Ballad of the Brown King*, see especially Jackson, "Margaret Bonds and *The Ballad of the Brown King*."
32. Yale JWJ 26, Box 16, folder 374: no. 207.
33. Ada Meseleff for Sam Fox Publishing Company (New York) to Langston Hughes (New York) (Yale JWJ MSS 26, Box 16, folder 375, no. 267).
34. See Craig Prentiss, "Simon of Cyrene and Signifying Race in Early 20th Century African-American Theatre," *Ecumenica* 9 (2016): 21–37.
35. Countee Cullen, "Simon the Cyrenian Speaks," *Poetry* 24, no. 2 (1924): 76.
36. Yale JWJ 26, Box 16, folder 378: no. 348.
37. The modern recognition that Christ himself was probably Black, or at least on the dark-skinned side of what W. E. B. Du Bois had termed "the world color line," does not seem to have occurred to Hughes and Bonds, or to have been a part of their world's view of the biblical narrative.
38. Georgetown University Bonds Papers, shelfmark GTM-130530, Box 11, folder 1.
39. See Allegra Martin, "Expressions of African American Identity in the Cantata *Simon Bore the Cross* by Margaret Bonds and Langston Hughes" (DMA diss., University of Illinois at Urbana-Champaign, 2019), 120.

40. Manuscripts, Archives and Rare Books Division, Schomburg Center for Research in Black Culture, The New York Public Library, Margaret Bonds Papers shelfmark MG873, Box 7, folder 10.

41. Hortense Love, African American soprano who commissioned Bonds's *Five Creek-Freedmen Spirituals* in 1941.

42. *Tambourines to Glory*, a "gospel singing play" by Langston Hughes based on his collection of poems by the same name, performed with music by Jobe Huntley (1917–95).

43. Bonds (New York) to Hughes (New York), September 6, 1964 (Columbia College, Chicago, Helen Walker-Hill papers, Box 5, Series 4, folder 8.5).

44. Rorem discusses his relationship with Bonds in his 1994 memoir *Knowing When to Stop* (New York: Simon & Schuster, 1994).

45. Bonds (New York) to Rorem (n.p.), June 21, 1966 (Columbia College, Chicago, Helen Walker-Hill papers, Box 5, Series 4, folder 8.2).

46. Bonds to Rorem, July 4, 1966 (Columbia College, Chicago, Helen Walker-Hill papers, Box 5, Series 4, folder 8.2). The book in question is *The Paris Diary of Ned Rorem* (London: Barrie & Rockliff, 1966), and Rorem may have thought that Bonds would be "appalled" by it because in it he publicly and unapologetically came out as gay, scandalizing much of the musical world.

47. Bonds to Rorem, July 7, 1967 (Columbia College, Chicago, Helen Walker-Hill papers, Box 5, Series 4, folder 8.2).

48. A two-page manuscript "detailed description" of *The Montgomery Variations*, "on the stationery of an L.A. institution," signed by Bernstein, "who may have been sent this outline in hopes that he would conduct it," has been advertised as being for sale through the Soho bookstore Nudel Books, through Abe Books. See https://bit.ly/3oaanWV (accessed March 1, 2021). My thanks to Mr. Anthony E. Philpott (Raleigh, North Carolina) for bringing this item to my attention.

49. "Alumni News" item dated December 18, 1967 from the Margaret Bonds file of the Northwestern University Libraries (Northwestern University Archives).

50. For McShee's performance, see https://bit.ly/3H2a86X (accessed July 29, 2021); concerning the Nashville Symphony Young People's Concerts, January 23 and 24, 2020, see https://bit.ly/3mCrgsC (accessed July 5, 2020).

51. See "Selections from *Montgomery Variations* – Margaret Bonds," *Hollywood Bowl*, https://bit.ly/3KwVXaL (accessed July 29, 2021).

52. Bonds (New York) to Hughes (New York), November 23, 1966 (Yale JWJ 26, Box 17, folder 382).

2

HOPE, DIVINE BENEVOLENCE,
AND *THE MONTGOMERY VARIATIONS*

It is widely repeated that *The Montgomery Variations* of Margaret Bonds – a seven-movement set of programmatic variations for orchestra based on the spiritual "I Want Jesus to Walk with Me" – was written for or inspired by "the freedom march" led by Martin Luther King, Jr., that took place in March 1965.[1] These accounts are false.

In fact, as we have seen, Bonds's correspondence shows that she played the completed work for Raoul Abdul in September 1964, five months before the first plans were laid for the Selma-to-Montgomery marches.[2] The urban legend (more than this it is not) is unfortunate not only because it is untrue, but also because it obscures the work's position in Bonds's creative life and its direct connection to her personal experiences with the Jim Crow South. Worse, the erroneous assignment implicitly devalues the actual subjects of *The Montgomery Variations* as Bonds details these in the programs she tendered for the work.

It is an extraordinary composition born of an extraordinary year. Most generally, in 1964 the United States and the world were still reeling from the assassination of President John F. Kennedy on November 22, 1963 – an assassination that, apart from its own inherent tragedy, threw into turmoil a US social landscape that was already fraught with conflict and violence, including the steadily escalating casualties of the Vietnam War. The new US president, Lyndon B. Johnson, used his power and his awareness of the critical state of race relations in the United States to champion the Civil Rights Act of 1964, a piece of landmark legislation that would, finally, begin to enforce the Fourteenth Amendment to the Constitution, assuring equal protection under the laws to all persons in US jurisdiction. That law represented a vital step forward for the more than ten million African Americans living in the United States at the time, but it also fueled White rage directed at the victims of state-sanctioned hatred and oppression. Angry segregationists took to violence in the streets even as White politicians with millions of supporters blamed Blacks themselves for the ghettos and segregated housing they were forced to live in, the unemployment that kept them in perpetual poverty, and the inferior school systems that provided the only education accessible to poor Black youth. Police pledged to protect and serve engaged in new brutalities that, in turn, sparked widespread riots.

But there was also hope – for the summer of 1964 was the "Freedom Summer" – a concerted effort by northern anti-racist activists to challenge the exclusion of Blacks from the political process in Mississippi. Although that campaign ultimately managed to add only about 1,600 names of newly registered Blacks to the voting rolls, it led to the establishment of "Freedom Schools" around Mississippi, persuaded more than 17,000 African Americans to register to vote, and ultimately paved the way for the Voting Rights Act of 1965.

The year 1964 was also significant in other, more obviously artistic ways that bore materially on *The Montgomery Variations*. For one, because it was the centennial of the birth of German composer Richard Strauss (d. 1949), the airwaves, bookstores, concert halls, recording industry, musical press, and even popular press were flooded with contributions that sought to come to terms with that brilliant but highly problematic composer and his significance – a situation whose influence on *The Montgomery Variations* we shall explore later in this chapter.[3] For another, in 1964 the collaborative friendship between Margaret Bonds and Langston Hughes entered its twenty-eighth year.[4] As it did, the ambitiousness of Bonds's musical imagination increased, especially where projects centered on racial justice were concerned. And Bonds's renown, already great, continued to grow. *The Ballad of the Brown King*, *The Negro Speaks of Rivers*, and her *Freeman-Creek Spirituals* were widely performed, and she was in demand as performer, composer, and public speaker. Indicative of this renown is that in August 1964 she was featured in an important article/interview by Christina Demaitre in the

Washington Post titled: "She Has a Musical Mission: Developing Racial Harmony; Heritage Motivates Composing Career."[5]

Margaret Bonds would play *The Montgomery Variations* for Raoul Abdul within a month of that interview's publication. Demaitre could not have grasped the richness and complexity of the tapestry of personal motivations that propelled Bonds to the extraordinary life and creative personality that she was interviewing – not only her race, but also her sense of historical responsibility and consequence, her pride in the maternal heritage and staunchly feminist spirit, and her passionate commitment to the cause of global equality. But Demaitre's term *harmony* is an accurate one, in its ancient Greek philosophical sense (applied also to music) of "a unification of things that appear on a lower level to be dissimilar or unrelated or lacking in order."[6] Addressing itself to a politically and racially fraught world, *The Montgomery Variations* is a deeply philosophical musical "unification" of strands ranging from African American spirituals to European concert music, to blues, gospel, and jazz. The programs Bonds wrote for the work show that these disparate threads musically chronicle the struggle for racial equality in the South during the period 1955–63, characterize those events themselves and their participants, and comment on them. Ultimately, *The Montgomery Variations* offers a closing vision of a peace and a reconciliation that were very much still things of the future in Bonds's time (as indeed they remain today).

The Programs

Bonds wrote two programs explaining the music of *The Montgomery Variations*. Neither is dated, but one appears to respond to points in Rorem's letter of July 4, 1966 (see p. 50), and thus may be assigned a date later than that; this program also was evidently written for a concert that would have paired *The Montgomery Variations* with *The Ballad of the Brown King*. The earlier, more detailed program may be the one that Bonds mentioned to Rorem on June 21, 1966. The two programs are presented side by side in Figure 2.1.

Original Program (June 21, 1966, or earlier) (Manuscripts, Archives and Rare Books Division, Schomburg Center for Research in Black Culture, The New York Public Library, Margaret Bonds Papers shelfmark MG873, Box 7, folder 1).	Revised Program (after July 4, 1966) (Booth Family Center for Special Collections, Georgetown University Libraries, Washington, DC, shelfmark GTM-130530, Box 5, folder 6).
	"The Montgomery Variations" is a group of freestyle variations based on the Negro Spiritual theme, "I want Jesus to Walk with Me." The treatment suggests the manner in which Bach constructed his partitas – a bold statement of the theme, followed by variations of the theme in the same key – major and minor.
	Because of the personal meanings of the Negro spiritual themes, Margaret Bonds always avoids over-development of the melodies.
	"The Montgomery Variations" were written after the composer's visit to Montgomery, Alabama, and the surrounding area in 1963 (on tour with Eugene Brice and the Manhattan Melodaires[7]).

(cont.)

In December 1960, "The Ballad of the Brown King" was dedicated to Martin Luther King, Jr., and presented at Clark Center, YWCA in New York, by the Church of the Master and Clark Center as a benefit to [the] Southern Christian Leadership Conference. Langston Hughes, the author of the text, was present on this occasion.

THE MONTGOMERY VARIATIONS

I Decision

Under the leadership of Martin Luther King Jr and SCLC, Negroes in Montgomery decided to boycott the bus company and to fight for their rights as citizens.

I. DECISION

The Negro decides to rise against his oppressors. The Negro in America is a Judeo-Christian. Though, in many instances[,] his religion is unenlightened, deep in his unconscious is an unshakeable faith in God, the Father, and in his "only begotten son," Jesus. In his most courageous stand against his oppressors, then, it is the faith in the Divine Intelligence which enables him to employ the methods of Passive Resistance — and thereby martyr himself for the Cause of Brotherhood and Democracy.

II. PRAYER MEETING

Before the Bus Boycott the Negro calls on God. As all Negroes in America, the Negroes in Montgomery gathered in their churches to pray – some in eloquent silence, and others releasing themselves of their repressions with tambourines and shouting, and in many Negro church meetings there is always one sister or brother who cannot restrain himself from resorting to body gesticulations including lifting his arms to Heaven and beating his feet – many times marching up and down the aisles of the church, unrestrainedly exhibiting his humility to Almighty God, as well as to the assembled worshippers.

III. MARCH

"If Jesus Goes With Me I'll Go." "Blessed Assurance, Jesus is Mine." As the early Christians, now the Negroes of Montgomery were willing to be thrown to the lions. Jesus, walking with them, they refused to ride on segregated buses.

"Love Ye One Another," no violence, but no longer would they be subservient to their white brothers. Thus, a steady, determined walking to their jobs to earn their daily bread.

II Prayer Meeting

Trut [sic] to custom prayer meetings precedes [sic] their action. Prayer meetings start quietly with humble petitions to God. During the course of the meeting, members siezed [sic] with religious fervor shout and dance. Oblivious to their fellow worshippers [sic] they exhibit their love of God and their Faith in Deliverance by gesticulation, clapping and beating their feet.

III March

The Spirit of the Nazarene marching with them, the Negroes of Montgomery walked to their work rather than be segregated on the buses. The entire world, symbolically with them, marches.

(cont.)

IV. DAWN IN DIXIE

Montgomery is no isolated town. Montgomery became a focal point of the world. The entire South, "Dixie[,]" began to wake up that something new was happening. Change, no matter how painful[,] is in the Divine Plan. There is honeysuckle, magnolias, and Spanish Moss hanging from trees it destroys. Spanish Moss is a parasite – miles of it are depressing. Swamps are foreboding. Perhaps one day then, even the camelias known as "Pink Perfection" laugh at the people of the South. The "Dawn in Dixie" caused all of America to awaken.

V. ONE SUNDAY IN THE SOUTH

What is meant by "Southern die-hards?" [*sic*] The Negroes were having such a good time praising God and Jesus one Sunday morning in Alabama. (The trumpet announces "I Want Jesus to Walk With Me," in a major key.) Little children were being taught Faith and to love their neighbors. Die-hards planted a bomb in the church to teach Negroes their place.

IV Dawn[8] in Dixie

Dixie, the home of the Camelias [*sic*] known as "pink perfection," magnolias, jasmine and Spanish moss, awakened to the fact that something new was happening in the South.

V One Sunday in the South

Children were in Sunday School learning about Jesus, the Prince of Peace. Southern "die-hards" planted a bomb and several children were killed.

VI. LAMENT
In the Passive Resistance Movement one does not resort to violence. "Vengeance is mine sith [*recte* sayeth] the Lord." One cries, moans and groans and calls for help from the Mother-Father God. Here the theme is stated simply, with little decoration, with [the] exception of a few embellishments natural to Negro improvisation in their churches of the primitive type.
The few embellishments employed are natural to Negroes, and may be heard in their churches of the primitive type.

[No program for "Benediction" in this document]

VI Lament
The world *was* shaken by the cruelty of the Sunday School bombing. Negroes, as usual[,] leaned on their Jesus to carry them through this crisis of grief and humiliation.

VII Benediction
A benign God, Father and Mother to all people, pours forth Love to His children – the good and the bad alike.

Figure 2.1 Original and revised programs for *The Montgomery Variations*.

Considered individually and together, these programs offer valuable general insights into Bonds's conception of the *Variations*. The titles for the first six movements are identical in both programs, but the earlier program explains the work in philosophical and religious terms while the later one translates those ideas into concrete terms that focus on specific events with which performers and listeners would more readily identify, explaining the connections between *The Montgomery Variations*, Bonds's two tours of the Southern states,[9] *The Ballad of the Brown King*, Langston Hughes, Martin Luther King, Jr., and the civil rights campaign of the Southern Christian Leadership Conference. The biggest difference between the two, however, is the absence of a program for Movement VII ("Benediction") in the earlier program – a difference that, as we shall see, probably reflects the dramatic events of the quest for racial justice in the United States between September 1963 and the summer of 1964.

A few preliminary comments on these two documents are necessary. First, the later program contains a few factual errors that might be dismissed as the products of poetic license, but in view of the seriousness of the subject and the social project with which it engaged probably resulted instead from incomplete and otherwise flawed information available to Bonds at the time. Most important among these problems is Bonds's portrayal of the Montgomery bus boycott as the result of a decision taken by the Southern Christian Leadership Conference (SCLC) under the direction of Martin Luther King, Jr. In fact, the SCLC was not founded until January 10, 1957, several weeks after the boycott's end; it was the result of the boycott's success, not the cause of it. The boycott was actually organized and coordinated throughout by a women's group in Montgomery, the Women's Political Council, under the leadership of Jo Ann Gibson Robinson (1912–92).[9] King was involved with the campaign, but this involvement was through the Montgomery Improvement Association, which was formed (with King as president) by Black ministers and community leaders in Montgomery four days after the arrest of Rosa Parks, on December 5, 1955. In other words, King had no direct role in the decision to undertake the boycott.

Second, as mentioned above, the *Variations* were not "written for" or otherwise tied to any of the marches from Selma to Montgomery that took place in March 1965: the date on the autograph predates those marches, and the programs do not refer to them.

Third, *The Montgomery Variations* were instead directly inspired by Bonds's own experiences during two performance tours that took her into the Jim Crow South. Although the surviving documentation is filled with gaps, it does reveal that in 1963 (the year cited in the second program) the group traveled to Raleigh, North Carolina (March 19), Knoxville, Tennessee (April 4), Birmingham, Alabama (April 5), and Pensacola, Florida (March 31); by April 7 they were in Akron, Ohio, out of the South.[10] That tour was evidently successful enough for the same group to undertake a second tour in 1964. That tour, which began on March 12, took them first to Asheville, North Carolina, for several days,[11] then to Beaufort, South Carolina (March 17)[12] and "the South Carolina Islands with their moss-laden trees," Columbia, South Carolina (March 18), and Atlanta, Georgia.[13] The tour also included performances in Albany, Georgia (March 22), Montgomery, Alabama (March 23), Greenville, South Carolina (March 24), Decatur, Alabama (March 25), Meridian and Natchez, Mississippi (March 26 and 27), Austin, Texas (March 30), Oklahoma City, Oklahoma (April 1), Wichita, Kansas (April 1), Lafayette, Indiana (April 3), Nashville, Tennessee (April 6),[14] Indianapolis, Indiana (April 8), and Cleveland, Ohio (April 10). By April 11, Bonds was able to write to Hughes again from New York.[15]

Fourth, because virtually every one of the stations in the group's Southern tours was a flashpoint in the Civil Rights Movement in the 1950s and early 1960s, the conditions and circumstances Bonds encountered during those tours may be fairly said to have given her firsthand experience with the increasingly tense and volatile racial climate of the South. This intersection of personal experience and social climate may well have led to her decision to use two major moments of the Civil Rights Movement as the inspiration for the *Variations*: (1) the Montgomery bus boycotts (December 5, 1955–December 20, 1956); and (2) the Sixteenth Street Baptist Church bombing (September 15, 1963).

Fifth, and more generally, the *Variations* situate those two events in the midst of the courage and faith of the African Americans whose boycott cost the public transit system between 30,000 and 40,000 fares each day, with losses of USD $250,000 to

Montgomery Bus Lines (nearly USD $2.5 billion in 2021), several thousand dollars in taxes to the City of Montgomery, and several million dollars in lost business to White businesses.[16] Their bravery and strategy inflicted on the city's segregated busing system a 75 percent loss of transit funds, which forced the bus line to cease transportation over the Christmas holiday and lay off employees – a situation that imposed further losses on the merchants who lost business because of the transit shutdown. Bonds also emphasizes the goodwill of the millions internationally who observed and supported the boycotts ("The entire world, symbolically with them, marches," No. III), and the flowering of goodwill and desire for progress in the wake of the boycott's success (No. IV). This international support is echoed in No. VI ("Lament"), as "the world" is shaken by the Sixteenth Street Baptist Church bombing – although the second program for this movement makes clear that even with that support African Americans still turned not to "the world," but to their own communities and "their Jesus" for support in their "crisis of grief and humiliation."

These circumstances demonstrate that the experiences that inspired *The Montgomery Variations* were suffused with violence – and the first program makes clear Bonds's own commitment to the program of nonviolence that the Montgomery bus boycott represented. This is the context that makes the decision to launch the boycott (No. I) a turn of events dramatic and courageous, and this in turn explains the character of Bonds's music. It explains why a prayer meeting (No. II) was called for, and why the atmosphere of that prayer meeting, as described in Bonds's music, is extraordinarily tense, filled with worry and foreboding as well as exclamations of faith. Indeed, the climate of the Montgomery bus boycott, like that of the South as a whole, presented a largely uninterrupted barrage of harassment, bullying, and death threats to supporters of racial integration while it was in progress (No. III), and it continued – indeed, escalated – afterward. Neither was the violence by any means limited to Montgomery, nor did it by any means cease – a fact pointedly reflected in the tragic ending of No. V and the moving lament of No. VI. Violence and racist hatred were the quintessential ingredients of the social issues that Bonds addressed in *The Montgomery Variations*.

Finally, the programs and music implicitly but powerfully assert that although racism and hatred are widespread, the quest for racial justice is divinely mandated and universal and, with courageous resistance from the communities of oppressed African Americans, will eventually triumph. In Bonds's telling, the first two movements are clearly centered on Montgomery, and by the end of the third movement "the entire world" is watching. The scene of No. IV is "Dixie" (i.e., the South), not just Montgomery, and No. V depicts the Sunday School bombing that took place not in Montgomery, but in Birmingham, some ninety miles away. The revised program for No. VI speaks of the Black community and "the world," and No. VII ("Benediction"), with no specified location, predicts an outpouring of divine benevolence for all people, "the good and the bad alike."

The Music: A Synoptic Overview

The later program and Bonds's correspondence identify two musical foundations for *The Montgomery Variations*: the spiritual "I Want Jesus to Walk with Me" and the "partitas" of J. S. Bach. Although there were also significant other influences on the *Variations*, as we shall see, the spiritual and Bach warrant brief discussion here.

"I Want Jesus to Walk with Me" was not one of the most popular freedom songs used during the Montgomery bus boycotts.[17] That circumstance is also telling, for that spiritual *was* an unofficial anthem of the Birmingham Campaign of King, the SCLC, and the Alabama Christian Movement for Human Rights – a campaign that used marches on City Hall, mass meetings, lunch-counter sit-ins, and a boycott of downtown merchants just before Easter (the second-largest shopping holiday of the year) in order to compel the deeply segregated city of Birmingham to desegregate. The project began on April 3 and lasted until mid-September – but Bonds was in Birmingham for a concert on April 5, 1963, just as this difficult campaign was getting started: she personally felt its atmosphere fraught with threats of White-on-Black violence, witnessed the protesters' resolve and anticipation, and heard the ubiquitous singing of spirituals. Her program's foregrounding of King

Figure 2.2 First page of score of *The Montgomery Variations*. Booth Family Center for Special Collections, Georgetown University Libraries, Washington, DC, shelfmark GTM-130530, Box 12, folder 8. Used by permission.

and the Southern Christian Leadership Conference for the Montgomery bus boycott even though the SCLC was not formed until after that boycott may well reflect the fact that she looked at the

Alabama civil rights campaigns through the lens of that organization – and the ubiquity of "I Want Jesus to Walk with Me" in both the Birmingham campaign and *The Montgomery Variations* is probably a telltale sign of that perspective on her part.

The origins of "I Want Jesus to Walk with Me" are unclear. It does not occur in any nineteenth-century collections of African American song or any of known programs or recordings of the Fisk Jubilee Singers or other gospel quartets that were released in the first twenty-five years of the new century. In the minor mode, it was first recorded on October 2, 1926, by Homer Quincy Smith (1902–?) and released as the flip side of his single *Go Down, Moses* in 1927 – there, however, with the printed title "I Want Jesus to *Talk* with Me," even though Smith actually sings "I Want Jesus to *Walk* with Me" (emphasis added).[18] The former text and title are attached to the major-mode tune in a collection of spirituals from Covington, Georgia, titled *The Old Songs Hymnal: Words and Melodies from the State of Georgia* ([New York]: Century) and edited by Dorothy Bolton and Harry T. Burleigh.[19] By the time Bonds used it in *The Montgomery Variations* the song was widely published, performed, and recorded, including a recording by legendary contralto Marian Anderson and a setting for piano solo by Florence Price.[20]

Moreover, Bonds herself contributed to this discourse in two still-unpublished settings. The simpler of these, undated, is scored for four-part chorus with piano and, according to the autograph cover sheet, was written "for seventh and eighth grades."[21] The other, invited by cellist Kermit Moore and premiered by him in Princess Anne, Maryland, with an unidentified soprano and pianist on September 10, 1964,[22] is an arrangement of No. VI ("Lament") for solo high voice, cello, and piano, now titled simply *Walk with Me*.[23] Although the setting in *The Montgomery Variations* (see Ex. 2.1) of course carries no text, because the length and lyrics of spirituals vary widely from one iteration to the next it is useful to know that in *Walk with Me* Bonds used the following text:

> I want Jesus to walk with me,
> I want Jesus to walk with me,
> All along my pilgrim's journey
> I want Jesus to walk with me.

Example 2.1 *The Montgomery Variations*, I: "I Want Jesus to Walk with Me" (theme).

In my trials, Lord, walk with me,
In my trials, Lord, walk with me,
When the shades of life are falling
I want Jesus to walk with me.

In my troubles, Lord, walk with me,
In my troubles, Lord, walk with me,
When my life becomes a burden
I want Jesus to walk with me.

Bonds's program also describes her "treatment" of the spiritual as reminiscent of "the manner in which Bach constructed his partitas – a bold statement of the theme, followed by variations of the theme in the same key – major and minor," and explains that "[b]ecause of the personal meanings of the Negro spiritual themes, Margaret Bonds always avoids over-development of the melodies." These statements align *The Montgomery Variations* with the music of J. S. Bach, both directly and indirectly. Directly, the term "partita" technically denotes any sectional instrumental (usually keyboard) composition, but in connection with J. S. Bach and the German late baroque it also suggests that the series of movements will all be in the same key, varying only in mode. At the same time, while "Bach's partitas" was the usual Anglophone designation for the four volumes of the *Clavier-Übung*, only the fourth of those partitas, the *Goldberg Variations* (BWV 830), is laid out as a theme and variations. (That the *Goldberg Variations* would have been on Bonds's mind when the *Montgomery Variations* were composed is understandable, since by 1963 Glenn Gould's 1955 recording had assumed near-legendary status.[24])

Indirectly, these statements further align *The Montgomery Variations* with Bach via Bonds's contemporaneous chorale

The Music: A Synoptic Overview

cantata *Simon Bore the Cross* (see Chapter 1), which, in the tradition of Bach's chorale cantatas, treats the theme – in that case, the spiritual "And He Never Said a Mumblin' Word" – as a cantus firmus that remains relatively stable throughout, even as the character of the surrounding material varies widely in accordance with the changing emotions and developing significance of the words and situations. *Simon* also concurs with *The Montgomery Variations* in that both works topically and musically affirm the historical consequentiality of the legacies of Black folk – *Simon* through its celebration of Simon of Cyrene, and *The Montgomery Variations* through its celebration of the courage of African Americans and assurance that, through Jesus, walking with the boycotters, God was on the side of those who were fighting for racial justice. Most symbolically, both *Simon Bore the Cross* and *The Montgomery Variations* explore the agency of Black identity in a spiritual procession toward redemption – *Simon* through the procession to the crucifixion by which Christ absorbed and atoned for humanity's sin, and *The Montgomery Variations* through the marches and the unswerving procession of courage and good will through which racial justice and peace will one day be achieved, as "[a] benign God, Father and Mother to all people, pours forth Love to His children – the good and the bad alike."

Margaret Bonds used these historical, programmatic, and stylistic parameters as the foundation for a work of great stylistic eclecticism. The music of its seven movements is laid out as follows:

    I. "Decision" (*andante deciso*, ♩ = 92; 68 mm.): This movement is in D minor and cast in ternary form. The opening gesture is a dramatic *crescendo* beginning at *fortissimo* in the timpani and double basses, followed by a statement of "I Want Jesus to Walk with Me" in the brass, punctuated by hammer-stroke chords in the strings and woodwinds. The central section, *mezzo forte*, is on the dominant, A major, repeats motives from the theme in a gradual *crescendo*, leading to a final restatement of the theme in the brass, now accompanied by rushing ascents in the woodwinds and strings.

   II. "Prayer Meeting" (*religioso*, ♩ = 88 – *con moto*, ♩ = 104; 99 mm.). Cast in ternary form, this movement begins and ends in F major, but the entire main section alternates fluidly between D major and

D minor. Its subject, as Bonds describes it, is the distinctly African American form of communal worship that W. E. B. Du Bois and others have termed "the frenzy." The movement's introduction and conclusion are cast as an expectant and "shimmering" (Bonds's description in the score) F-major sonority with added *D, pianissimo*, with delicate shards of melody tossed about in the woodwinds. But the main body of the movement is a study in what Du Bois called "a people's sorrow, despair, and hope," pent-up and poised to erupt.[25] It begins with a paraphrase of the spiritual "Angels Watchin' over Me," which first appeared in James Rosamond Johnson's *Utica Jubilee Singers Hymnal* and is frequently performed with the exclamation "Lordy!" at the end of the second phrase – an exclamation that Bonds evokes instrumentally (Ex. 2.2a).[26] This then yields to a pedal-point *D* with rhythmic trochaic punctuations alternating on strong and weak beats in various accompanying instruments; a persistent tambourine is evocative of jewelry jingling as hands are clapped. The foreground of the movement is dominated by the woodwinds' and upper strings' recitativelike melodic interjections whose blue thirds and fluid rhythms give the character of spontaneous, improvisatory outbursts, but there are also sporadic solo interjections of the first few notes ("I want Jesus") of the spiritual, as well as one forceful statement of the first phrase, followed by a jazz-influenced paraphrase thereof (Ex. 2.2c). The climax of the movement combines these individual instrumental shoutings with a chordal passage in the brass that Bonds directs to be played "as an organ" (Ex. 2.2d).

III. "March" ($\lrcorner$ = 100, 78 mm.). This movement foregrounds counterpoint, representing the polyphonic interplay of different agencies in the bus boycott – including the marchers, as well as the shouting of their supporters and hecklers, along with the violence. It begins with a sturdy march melody in two-part counterpoint, then combines this with lyrical countermelodies entrusted to the three flutes. In m. 29, the violins introduce the spiritual theme in combination with this material (Ex. 2.3a). The movement builds to a tense climax with brass fanfares reminiscent of battle calls, and then to a restatement of the combined thematic elements with agitated string figures, *fortissimo*, as the marching Black workers, "the world march[ing] with them," courageously face shouting and violence from the segregationist White community. The movement ends quietly – but not before a paraphrase of the opening phrases of the spiritual return, followed by a cadential recitative that celebrates the workers' Black vernacular styles (Ex. 2.3b).

IV. "Dawn in Dixie" (no tempo given; 73 mm.). The later program's description of "Dixie" as "the home of the Camelias [*sic*] known as 'pink perfection,' magnolias, jasmine and Spanish moss" recalls

Example 2.2 *The Montgomery Variations,* II: (a) mm. 18–21; (b) mm. 50–56; (c) mm. 59–64, trombone solo; (d) mm. 81–85.

Example 2.3 *The Montgomery Variations,* III: (a) mm. 28–33; (b) mm. 67–73.

language from Bonds's first surviving letter to Langston Hughes written during the 1964 Southern tour: "[W]e drove out of the South Carolina islands with their moss-laden trees (camelias [*sic*] given me by gracious Southern ladies both colored and white)"[27] And indeed, the fragrantly beautiful Southern foliage is vividly suggested in No. IV, thanks to sensually exoticized woodwind writing redolent of Rimsky-Korsakov's *Scheherazade.* Written in the style of a chaconne based on an ostinato descending tetrachord – a musical figure emblematic of lament – the movement is cast in two strophes, each based on a plaintive, songlike melody whose incipit derives from that of "I Want Jesus to Walk with Me (Ex. 2.4a). Each

Example 2.4 *The Montgomery Variations*, IV: (a) mm. 9–22; (b) mm. 58–69.

of these strophes culminates in a contrasting episode of exultant beauty and pathos (Ex. 2.4b).

Example 2.5 *The Montgomery Variations*, V: mm. 41–45.

V. "One Sunday in the South" (no tempo given; 55 mm.). This movement traverses considerable historical and affective ground, from the victory and widespread sense of hope, progress, and jubilation that followed the Montgomery bus boycotts to the violence and tragedy that continued to be inflicted on Black communities after the boycott's end. It begins in D major, with "I Want Jesus to Walk with Me" presented by the solo trumpet, accompanied by a rhythmic figure in the strings and light percussion. A contrasting *B* section retains the major-mode chord progression of the theme, but couples this with a new melody that recalls the first movement of J. S. Bach's Third Brandenburg Concerto (Ex. 2.5). These two themes are then combined in a jubilant reprise, with the spiritual now entrusted to the full brass section, accompanied by racing scalar figures in the strings such as commonly encountered in Tchaikovsky's music – but the rejoicing is abruptly cut off as a solo wood block, *forte*, takes over the rhythm of the countermelody. The next four bars are a *crescendo* from ***ppp*** to ***fff***, with a roll in the timpani eventually complemented by crashes in the bass drum and cymbals – a vivid depiction of deadly explosions that took the lives of Addie Mae Collins, Cynthia Wesley, Carole Robertson, and Carol Denise McNair in the basement of the Sixteenth Street Baptist Church in Birmingham, Alabama, on September 15, 1963.

VI. "Lament" (*Doloroso*, ♩ = 80; 53 mm.). In addition to the *Walk with Me* arrangement for voice, cello, and piano already mentioned, Bonds also later returned to this movement in a planned piece for piano and orchestra titled *Adoration of the Master*.[28] In *The Montgomery Variations* it begins *mezzo forte*, turns to *pianissimo*

The Music: A Synoptic Overview

Example 2.6 *The Montgomery Variations*, VI: mm. 32–39.

in m. 16, and remains *piano* and *mezzo piano* for most of the remainder; the basses are silent throughout. Bonds's program suggests two sections ("the whole world was shaken" and Blacks leaning on "their Jesus" to "carry them through this crisis of grief and humiliation"), but the movement is laid out in three sections, each presenting one full statement of "I Want Jesus to Walk with Me." The first section is a figured presentation of the theme in three-part counterpoint, scored for first violins, violas, and celli; the second, a statement in octaves with both violin sections, and cellos, and soulfully embellished cadences. The third section restates the spiritual in the celli and first bassoon, embellishing this with a new countermelody, harmonized, whose motives are drawn from the movement's original countermelody and the spiritual itself (Ex. 2.6).

VII. "Benediction" (*à volunté*, ♩ = 96, 106 mm.). Thematically and tonally, this is the most complex movement of the entire *Montgomery Variations* – not surprisingly, given that it has to traverse the terrain from the profound sorrow of No. VI to the vision of divine benevolence, peace, and love described in Bonds's program. The movement is based on four distinct melodic components: a measured, melancholy theme derived from that of the "Lament," an unsettled, songlike theme whose closing bars recall the incipit of "I Want Jesus to Walk with Me," a theme in F major that is obviously derived from the spiritual; and the spiritual itself. The opening bars are devoted to the first of these, which is combined with the second beginning in m. 6. A half-cadence in D minor then leads, via two fermatas, to a *fortissimo* climax using the F-major theme derived from the spiritual (presented "with much dignity") (Ex. 2.7a). After this first climax dissolves, the initial

65

Example 2.7 *The Montgomery Variations*, VII: (a) mm. 28–39; (b) mm. 74–86.

dialogue between the lamenting material and the F-major variant of
the spiritual returns – but this time the powerful *crescendo* to
D minor leads to a statement of "I Want Jesus to Walk with Me"
in its original form, entrusted to four horns and three trombones in

Example 2.7 (cont.)

octaves, *fortississimo*, supported by other winds as the upper strings retain the songlike theme (Ex. 2.7b). With this radiant climax achieved, the music calms, remaining in a peaceful F major to the end. Motives from the spiritual close the work *pianississimo*, with virtually the full orchestra sounding – a stroke that, as we shall see, tellingly recalls the close of Richard Strauss's *Tod und Verklärung*, Op. 24 (Death and transfiguration, 1889).

The Divine Mandate for Racial Justice and the Musical Heritage

The above remarks give some idea of the stylistic variety and compositional complexity of *The Montgomery Variations*. These issues, already discussed in some detail by Helen Walker-Hill,[29] require more extensive consideration than is possible here, but a few general observations are necessary.

The first of these observations has to do with the richness of the work's use of Black vernacular repertoires – chiefly spirituals, gospel, and blues, and (less overtly) jazz. The spirituals' influence is the most obvious of these, of course, mostly via the central "I Want Jesus to Walk with Me," but also via the short but meaningful reference to *Angels Watchin' over Me* in "Prayer Meeting" (see Ex. 2.2a, above). That same movement also includes a recitativelike trope on the spiritual, scored for trombone solo and suggestive of a male solo improvisation (Ex. 2.2c, above) as well as an important climax and ensuing recitative for the first violins; both of these celebrate the blue thirds typical of Black vernacular styles. As shown in Example 2.3b, above, a similar gesture occurs at the end of the march, designated first *molto ff e espressivo* and then "with great pathos." These and other such passages occur at climactic moments and in their aftermath – as summital enunciations of Black identity in music, via repertoires generally accepted as paradigmatic of that identity.

In Bonds's world – as also in the White-dominated establishment of concert music today – such musical pronouncements of Black identity were usually segregated out from the genres, techniques, and forms of classical music – the very things that provide their context in *The Montgomery Variations*. But Bonds does not acknowledge this segregation. Instead, she overtly integrates these stereotypically Black and White styles. The most obvious White idiom, of course, is the "partitas" of J. S. Bach, via the idea of the free variation-set that Bonds cites in the later program. But as shown in Figure 2.3, the influence of some of Bach's cantatas, the Credo of the B-minor Mass, and many of his later keyboard collections is also present in the mirror symmetry of the work's

I	II	III	IV	V	VI	VII
Decision	Prayer Meeting	March	Dawn in Dixie	One Sunday in the South	Lament	Benediction
Bold, literal statement of spiritual (D minor)	Reflective, slow A-B-A (F-d-F)	Lively, energetic; literal statement of spiritual (D minor)	Songlike, strophic, lamento bass; paraphrase of spiritual (D minor)	Lively, energetic; literal statement of spiritual (D major)	Reflective, slow, A-B-A; literal statement of spiritual (D minor)	Songlike theme→ F-major trope on spiritual → literal statement of spiritual in D minor in combination with other themes (D minor → F major)

Figure 2.3 Symmetrical layout of *The Montgomery Variations*.

large-scale plan – a symmetry that Bonds had also explored in *Simon Bore the Cross*. The outermost movements ("Decision" and "Benediction") state the cantus firmus boldly and in the main key, as do the outermost movements of *Christ lag in Todesbanden* (BWV 4) and *Wachet auf, ruft uns die Stimme* (BWV 140) and the "Prelude" and "Crucifixion" in *Simon Bore the Cross*. Nos. II and VI ("Prayer Meeting" and "Lament") are both reflective and slow, with clear tripartite designs, while Nos. III and V ("March" and "One Sunday in the South") are both outgoing, lively, energetic, and freer in form. And No. IV ("Dawn in Dixie") serves as the heart of the work – a movement in which the songlike style, strophic form, powerful climax near the end, and nearly complete absence of direct statement of the spiritual render it an ungrammaticality vis-à-vis the surrounding movements. Structurally, this memorable movement is a counterpart to the struggle between life and death in No. 3 of *Christ lag in Todesbanden*, verse two of the chorale ("Zion hört die Wächter singen") in *Wachet auf, ruft uns die Stimme*, and Mary's songful solo "Who Is that Man?" from *Simon Bore the Cross*.

This symmetry also establishes a hierarchy among the movements that reinforces the work's poetic and programmatic design, for the first component of each internal pair is preparatory to its consequent: the "Prayer Meeting" is the prerequisite of the "March," and the tragedy that disrupts the jubilation of "One Sunday in the South" is the raison d'être of the "Lament." And these movements are ensconced among others that serve, by means of their style and their position in the large-scale design, as programmatic and musical anchors for the whole. No. I articulates the power of courage and decisiveness among God's people as they undertake their nonviolent campaign for racial equality. No. IV gives central voice to a tender, soulful beauty that W. E. B. Du Bois (in a statement that Bonds would memorably celebrate in her setting of his *Credo*) had described as the beauty of genius, sweetness of soul, and "strength in that meekness which shall yet inherit this turbulent earth" of Black folk.[30] And No. VII, finally, restates the spiritual in its original tonic (D minor) but then breaks with the tonally closed cycles typical of earlier variation-based works. That tonal progression is telling, for this is a movement that looks from the turbulent present ridden with strife, violence, and sorrow to a future in which a benign God enables those on the side of right to transcend those evils. This movement's cycling between the F major first associated with "Prayer Meeting" with the D minor of "I Want Jesus to Walk with Me" and the racial strife that compelled Montgomery's Black population to walk to work in the boycott serves a poetic purpose – for when peace finally comes, at the end of the movement, it is in the prayerful F major that began and ended the work's "Prayer Meeting." The final moments of *The Montgomery Variations*, in breaking from the D minor associated with the strife that initiated the series of events in the work, submit a poetically symbolic moment in which Bonds's vision transcends the most obvious hypotexts that (per Bonds's program note) underlay the work.

That musical and poetic transcendence offers an insight into one final significant aspect of *The Montgomery Variations* – for this is a set of variations for orchestra, not keyboard, and that scoring aligns it also with other works that Bonds would have known such as Brahms's *Variations on a Theme of Haydn*, the finales of Beethoven's "Eroica" and Ninth Symphonies, and Richard Strauss's *Don Quixote*.[31] The Beethovenian counterparts are fitting archetypes for *The Montgomery Variations* because of their popularly understood narrative progress through struggle and strife to triumph and joy – a progress also vividly conveyed in Bonds's later program for her *Variations*. And the example of Richard Strauss, whose presence (as noted above) veritably saturated the Western musical world in 1964, would be material because *Don Quixote*, like the Lisztian tone poems that had preceded it, employed a process of thematic transformation dictated in large part by the needs of the work's underlying musical program – just as the transformations of "I Want Jesus to Walk with Me" in *The Montgomery Variations* are clear responses to the events outlined in the two programs Bonds wrote.

Strauss is also manifest in Bonds's transfigurative vision of Black–White relations in her *Variations* – not only through the transformations of the "I Want Jesus" theme itself, but also in the work's final bars. Strauss's *Tod und Verklärung* (Death and transfiguration), after a blazing peroration of the transfigured version of the theme from which the entire work proceeds, ends *pianissimo* but with virtually every instrument of the orchestra sounding, and Bonds's *Montgomery Variations* takes that one dynamic level further, with virtually every instrument sounding *pianississimo* in the work's final bars – an effect that, although difficult to pull off in performance, produces the fullest possible sound at the quietest possible dynamic level. For all the many and important differences in social status, musical aesthetics, and philosophical outlook between Richard Strauss and Margaret Bonds, in the final analysis the distance is not so very great between the moment when the soul of Strauss's protagonist leaves his body and "finds[s] perfected in the most glorious form in the eternal cosmos that which he could not fulfil here on earth"[32] and the envisioned future of Bonds's *Variations* in which "A benign God, Father and Mother to all people, pours forth Love to His children – the good and the bad alike."

Margaret Bonds's integration of these musical spheres and idioms that – especially in the White musical world – were usually segregated out from one another also points to one other crucial way in which *The Montgomery Variations* intersects with its hypotexts but ultimately departs from them. Margaret Bonds does not celebrate French generals and emperors or fictional noblemen of the Spanish Renaissance, nor does she musically impart peace and redemption to anonymized types such as the protagonist of *Death and Transfiguration*. Instead, the subjects valorized and ultimately vindicated in *The Montgomery Variations* are her own contemporaries, including all who support the cause of racial justice but especially African Americans. The heroes of the *Variations* are the countless poor and hereunnamed Blacks who undertook to challenge the segregation and systemic racism of their own day and managed, in battle after battle, through courage, determination, perseverance, strategy, and *faith*, to bring about meaningful social change, including the sweeping Civil Rights Act of 1964 that was signed into law on July 2, 1964, just as Bonds was completing her work on *The Montgomery Variations*. These countless unnamed persons, whom King several years later would herald as "the poor and despised of the twentieth century ... [who] will fight for human justice, brotherhood, secure peace and abundance for all,"[33] are the subjects who populate the programmatic and musical landscapes of *The Montgomery Variations*. They, in Bonds's musical vision, were to be the architects of a just future, the agents of God's will in ultimately achieving racial equality and lasting peace.

***

The racial harmony that Christina Demaitre described as Margaret Bonds's musical mission never came, but that did not deter Margaret Bonds. *The Montgomery Variations* would not be performed until 1967[34] – but within a year of its completion Margaret Bonds was at work on a new and even more ambitious piece. That new venture would further extend the project for racial justice and equality that had been born of her commitment to "go farther" than her mother and her ancestors to build on their work "for Mankind, for our oppressed Race."[35] It would take the form not of brilliant and powerful programmatic instrumental music, but rather of a musical social-justice creed that would bring together voices and instruments in the work of moving performers and listeners to action in the divinely mandated quest for global equality. Its text: the *Credo* of W. E. B. Du Bois.

Notes

1. The first such report seems to be found in Helen Walker-Hill, "Margaret Bonds," in her *From Spirituals to Symphonies: African-American Women Composers and Their Music* (Westport, CT: Greenwood, 2002), 174.

2. Bonds (New York) to Hughes (New York), September 6, 1964 (Columbia College, Chicago, Helen Walker-Hill papers, Box 5, Series 4, folder 8.5). There were actually three "freedom marches" from Selma to Montgomery, all in March 1965. All were occasioned by Alabama's voter-suppression laws and police violence against nonviolent demonstrations. The decision to march on the state capital, Montgomery, from Selma, about fifty-four miles away, was taken in response to an Alabama State Trooper's murder of Jimmie Lee Jackson, 26, on February 18, 1965, as he tried to protect his mother from a Trooper's nightstick when law enforcement attempted to disperse an evening march. The first "freedom march," which was widely publicized and came to be known as "Bloody Sunday," took place on March 7, 1965, and involved between 525 and 600 people; it was violently dispersed at the

Edmund Pettus Bridge by mounted police using clubs and tear gas. The second, involving about 2,000 people, took place on March 9, 1965, and went only as far as the Edmund Pettus Bridge, where the participants knelt and prayed in commemoration of the victims of the first march. The third march lasted from March 21 to March 25, 1965, and covered the entire distance, beginning with about three hundred marchers (per judicial order) and eventually growing to include about 25,000.

3. See, for example, "Strauss Today: His Centennial Prompts a Look at His Music," *New York Times* (October 18, 1964): X 11.

4. See especially Anna Harwell Celenza, *Margaret Bonds and Langston Hughes: A Musical Friendship* (Washington, DC: Georgetown University Library, 2016).

5. Christina Demaitre, "She Has a Musical Mission: Developing Racial Harmony; Heritage Motivates Composing Career," *The Washington Post* 87, no. 253 (August 14, 1964).

6. Thomas J. Mathiesen, "Harmonia and Ethos in Ancient Greek Music," *Journal of Musicology* 3 (1984): 264–79 at 266.

7. The exact dates of Bonds's work as accompanist with the Melodaires are not known; the group comprised seven male voices and, according to contemporary press reports, covered classical, folk, popular, and religious repertoires. Bass-baritone Eugene Brice (1913–80) was the most accomplished member, having performed in *Porgy and Bess* and Marc Blitzstein's *Regina* with the New York City Opera. The group was conducted by Willie Jonson, who at the time was assistant to Robert Shaw as New York City Opera's Choral Director.

8. The typescript gives "Down" instead of "Dawn" here, but the autograph score unambiguously gives "Dawn." "Down" appears to be another one of the several typos in the typed program note.

9. See *The Montgomery Bus Boycott and the Women Who Started It: The Memoir of Jo Ann Gibson Robinson*, ed. David J. Garrow (Knoxville: University of Tennessee Press, 1987).

10. *The News and Observer*, Raleigh, North Carolina (March 17, 1963): 53; *Knoxville Journal* (March 29, 1963): 30; *Birmingham News* (March 30, 1963): 64; *Pensacola News Journal,* Pensacola, Florida (March 30, 1963): 10; *Akron Beacon Journal* (March 6, 1963): 55.

11. Bonds (New York) to Hughes (New York), Yale JWJ 26, Box 16, folder 380: no. 450.

12. Bonds (Beaufort, South Carolina) to Larry Richardson and Djane Richardson (New York), Margaret Bonds papers of the Schomburg Center of the New York Public Library (shelfmark MG 873 Box 2, folder 7). Bonds outlined the stations of the 1964 tour, together with information on performance venues and local sponsors, in an

73

itinerary dated March 14, 1964 (Georgetown University Bonds Papers shelfmark GTM 130530 Box 4, folder 7).

13. Bonds (Atlanta) to Hughes (New York), March 19, 1964 (Yale JWJ 26, Box 16, folder 380: no. 451).

14. A postcard to Hughes from a Holiday Inn in Nashville, Tennessee, postmarked April 9, 1964, reports that she had been with John Wesley Work III, his wife, and Arna Bontemps in the latter's "own surroundings" (i.e., in Nashville, probably at Fisk University, where both Work and Bontemps were employed), and that she would be in Indianapolis that night, then "Cleveland and home" on April 10 (Yale JWJ MSS 26, Box 16, folder 380: no. 452).

15. Letter from Bonds in New York to Hughes in New York (Yale JWJ MSS 26, Box 16, folder 380: no. 453).

16. National Parks Service, "The Montgomery Bus Boycott (U.S. National Park Service)," accessed June 21, 2021, www.nps.gov/art icles/montgomery-bus-boycott.htm; Domenic J. Capeci, Jr., "From Harlem to Montgomery: The Bus Boycotts and Leadership of Adam Clayton Powell, Jr., and Martin Luther King, Jr.," *The Historian* 41 (1979): 721–37 at 730–31.

17. The most popular hymns and spirituals used during the Montgomery bus boycott were "Ain't Gonna Study War No More," "Hold On" (also known as "Keep Your Hand on the Plow" and "Keep Your Eyes on the Prize"), "I Got a Home in that Rock," "Leaning on the Everlasting Arms," "Lift Him Up," "Old Time Religion," "Onward, Christian Soldiers," "Poor Man Drives," "Shine on Me," "Steal Away," "Swing Low, Sweet Chariot," "This Little Light of Mine," and "We Are Soldiers in the Army." See Robert Darden, "Montgomery," in his *Nothing but Love in God's Water: Black Sacred Music from the Civil War to the Civil Rights Movement* (University Park: Pennsylvania State University Press, 2014), 119–35, *passim*.

18. Anthony Heilbut, cited in Robert M. Marovich, *A City Called Heaven: Chicago and the Birth of Gospel Music* (Urbana: University of Illinois Press, 2015), 55.

19. A four-part harmonization of the tune is found in Dorothy Bolton and Harry Burleigh, *Old Songs Hymnal: Words and Melodies from the State of Georgia* (New York: Century, 1929), no. 84. An ink transcription of the melody, evidently in Burleigh's hand, with typed lyrics that are similar to but not identical to that found in the *Old Songs Hymnal*, typed by Bolton, also survives. My thanks to Professor Brian Moon (University of Arizona) for sharing this information. On the *Old Songs Hymnal*, see Brian Alan Moon, "The *Old Songs Hymnal:* Harry Burleigh and His Spirituals during the Harlem Renaissance (PhD diss., University of Colorado–Boulder, 2006).

20. Marian Anderson, *He's Got the Whole World in His Hands: Spirituals*, RCA Victor Red Seal LSC2592 (1962); Florence B. Price, *Ten Negro*

Spirituals for the Piano, ed. John Michael Cooper (New York: G. Schirmer, 2020).

21. Margaret Bonds, *I Want Jesus to Walk with Me*, ed. John Michael Cooper (Worcester, MA: Hildegard Publishing, forthcoming). The autograph survives in the Beinecke Rare Book and Manuscript Library, Yale Collection of American Literature, James Weldon Johnson collection, Margaret Bonds papers (shelfmark JWJ 151, Box 4, folder 25). Citations to this Collection will henceforth be cited as "Yale JWJ 151," followed by the box number and folder number.

22. Letter from Bonds (New York) to Hughes (New York) (Yale JWJ 26, Box 16, folder 380: no. 474).

23. Margaret Bonds, *Walk with Me*, ed. John Michael Cooper (Worcester, MA: Hildegard Publishing, forthcoming). Georgetown University Bonds Papers, shelfmark GTM-130530 Box 11, folder 2.

24. On the cultlike status of Gould and his 1955 *Goldberg* recording, see Terry Teachout, "Gouldism," *Commentary* 114, no. 5 (2002): 61–64.

25. W. E. Burghardt Du Bois, *The Souls of Black Folk: Essays and Sketches*, 3rd ed. (Chicago: A. C. McClurg, 1903), 191.

26. J. Rosamond Johnson, *Utica Jubilee Singers Spirituals, as Sung at the Utica Normal and Industrial Institute of Mississippi* (Philadelphia, PA: Oliver Ditson, 1930), 4–5.

27. Bonds (Atlanta) to Hughes (New York), March 19, 1964 (Yale JWJ MSS 26, Box 16, folder 380: no. 451).

28. Yale JWJ 151 MSS, Box 8, folder 40.

29. See Walker-Hill, "Margaret Bonds," 156–58; Dartisha L. Mosley, "Margaret Bonds: Biography," *Women of Rosenwald: Curating Justice through the Arts (1928–1948)*, https://womenofrosenwald.omeka.net /exhibits/show/margaret-bonds/biography (accessed September 10, 2021); Anne Midgette, "A Forgotten Voice for Civil Rights Rises in Song at Georgetown," *The Washington Post* (November 10, 2017).

30. W. E. Burghardt Du Bois, *Darkwater: Voices from within the Veil* (New York: Harcourt, Brace and Howe, 1920), 3–4.

31. The surviving programs from Bonds's recitals of the early and mid-1930s, however, show that Robert Schumann's *Papillons* (Op. 2) – a work overtly based on thematic transformation – was among her favorite compositions. She performed it in recitals of November 9, 1931, April 15, 1934, and June 4, 1934 (Northwestern University Archives, Emily Boettcher Bogue [1907–1992] Papers, 19/3/6).

32. Letter from Richard Strauss to Friedrich von Hausegger, 1895; quoted from Willi Schuh, *Richard Strauss: A Chronicle of the Early Years, 1864–1898*, trans. Mary Whittall (Cambridge: Cambridge University Press, 1982), 180.

33. Martin Luther King, Jr., "A Testament of Hope (1968)," in *A Testament of Hope: Essential Writings and Speeches of Martin*

Luther King, Jr., ed. James Melvin Washington (New York: HarperCollins, 1991), 313–28 at 328.

34. "Alumni News" item dated December 18, 1967, from the Margaret Bonds file of the Northwestern University Libraries (Northwestern University Archives, Margaret Bonds file).

35. Letter from Margaret Bonds to Larry Richardson, December 17, 1942 (see Chapter 1, pp. 21–23).

3

THE TEXT AND MUSIC OF THE *CREDO*

As we shall see in Chapter 4, the *Credo* of W. E. B. Du Bois, first published in 1904 and revised in 1919–20, is part of a lineage of creeds and manifestos that spans a millennium and a half. That circumstance created special challenges for Du Bois because any contribution to a tradition-laden genre – whether in poetry, music, the visual arts, or scholarship – naturally places an onus on creators to position themselves within that lineage, clearly cognizant of its heritage and rhetorics but not derivative or epigonal. Du Bois's text reveals no Bloomian "anxiety of influence," motivated as that would be by the creator's need to overthrow the authority of his progenitors even as he avowed loyalty to them; nor is there any of what Sandra M. Gilbert and Susan Gubar, describing the historical-creative anxiety applicable to Victorian female authors (who were in a lower caste because of their sex) termed an "anxiety of authorship."[1] Rather, Du Bois seizes on historical models as stylistic points of departure, using them much like a "generic contract" – engendering expectations and guiding readers' perceptions of his meaning by the ways in which he adheres to and departs from those expectations.[2]

He did it boldly. Typically for creedal documents, Du Bois's *Credo* is cast as a series of short, discrete, but topically and circumstantially related professions of belief – statements that, typically for manifestos, outline and justify a program for sweeping societal reform. In publishing it, Du Bois publicly denied the sufficiency of the myriad creeds and manifestos already in existence and asserted that the implorations for social justice and global equality conveyed in his *Credo* were, despite its being authored by a member of a despised caste, worthy peers of its historical antecedents. That public act of defiance was all the bolder because this was the first overt contribution to that genre penned by an African American (indeed, aside from his own subsequent manifestos, it remained one of few such documents until the late 1960s).[3]

The challenge was further enhanced by Du Bois's own youth and station. When he penned and first published the *Credo*, in 1904,[4] he was just thirty-six years old, a rising and ambitious star in the heated and pressing discourse concerning Black Americans and race relations in the United States, and a professor at Atlanta University. His youth, stature, and institutional affiliation were significant, for all three generated professional tensions that in turned played out in the *Credo* itself. Atlanta University as a whole was what Du Bois would later term "the ivory tower of race"[5] – an institution that insisted, even amidst the Black Codes and deep in the heart of the Jim Crow South, that African Americans be afforded a superior and well-rounded liberal arts education equal to what was accessible to Whites. This contrasted starkly with the ideas of Booker T. Washington (1856–1915), twelve years Du Bois's senior and founder of the Tuskegee Institute some two hours away near Birmingham, Alabama. Washington and the Tuskegee Institute downplayed the evils of racism and taught that because African Americans had no generational history of societal enfranchisement, with its attendant responsibilities, they needed to acquire first of all an "industrial education" in so-called "useful trades," in order to strengthen their economic position before earning full equality and advancing to the fullness of a liberal arts education comparable to that of northern Whites.[6] For Washington and his supporters, Black folk had to prove themselves worthy of membership in White society.

The relationship between these two advocates for Black advancement, and the deterioration of their collaboration, warrants summary here. Nearly a decade before the *Credo*, at his graduation speech from Harvard, Du Bois had pronounced ideas that would have won Washington's approval – and indeed, in 1894 and 1897 Washington attempted to recruit Du Bois to Tuskegee (although these offers may have been partly motivated by a desire to bring Du Bois into his own fold and thus prevent the young star from upstaging him).[7] In 1899 the two collaborated on legal projects to protect Black voting rights in Georgia, and in 1900–1904 they again worked together in a challenge to segregation on railroad sleeping cars on the Southern Railroad. By then, however, the rising tide of racism had pushed Du Bois's own concept of race, and of the moral imperative for society to pursue racial equality, further and further away from Washington's own conspicuously accommodationist views. In 1896, in *Plessy v. Ferguson*, the US Supreme Court had declared segregation constitutional, and since then the Black Codes of the Jim Crow South had strengthened the oppression of US Black folk; the tide of White-on-Black violence, now not only accommodated by the law but in many ways prescribed by law, was spreading and deepening, with no end in sight. Those developments made the accommodationist tone of Washington's "Atlanta compromise," which had delighted Southern moderates and racists alike and been declared "the beginning of a moral revolution in America" by the editor of the *Atlanta Constitution*,[8] morally repugnant; and this strained the relationship between Du Bois and Washington beyond any realistic collaboration.

As a result of this deterioration, by 1903 – the year before the *Credo*'s first publication – Du Bois was compelled to publicly criticize Washington in *The Crisis*, noting with searing factual accuracy that

Mr. Washington distinctly asks that black people give up, at least for the present, three things –

> First, political power,
> Second, insistence on civil rights,
> Third, higher education of Negro youth –

And concentrate all their energies on industrial education, the accumulation of wealth, and the conciliation of the South. . . . As a result of this tender of the palmbranch, what has been the return? In these years there have occurred:

1. The disfranchisement of the Negro.
2. The legal creation of a distinct status of civil inferiority for the Negro.
3. The steady withdrawal of aid from institutions for the higher training of the Negro.[9]

By 1935, some twenty years after Washington's death and fifteen years after the publication of the *Credo* at the head of *Darkwater*, Du Bois had come to describe Washington's tactics in damning terms: referring to an episode that had occurred in a Pullman car shortly before Washington's death, he wrote:

There is a point where such sacrifice becomes cowardice; where meek submission becomes crime; . . . yet this incident throws curious and revealing light on the controversy which may always envelope the meaning of Booker T. Washington to America.[10]

By the time Du Bois published "The Social Significance of Booker T. Washington" in 1935, Margaret Bonds had already embarked on her own artistic quest to advocate for social justice. She had received her bachelor's and master's degrees in music (piano) at Northwestern University. She had worked closely with renowned soprano, actor, and activist Abbie Mitchell, who after Washington's death had served on the faculty of the Tuskegee Institute from 1931 to 1934. She had found deep inspiration in Langston Hughes's poem "The Negro Speaks of Rivers." The following year (1936) she would finally meet the poet and with him embark on a thirty-year collaborative friendship that would center on causes that resonated deeply with Du Bois's views, and in 1938 she would found the Allied Arts Academy in Chicago, which was dedicated to providing high-quality education in the arts to underprivileged youth. Her setting of the Du Bois *Credo*, originally written for soloists, chorus, and piano in 1964–66 and expanded to include orchestra in 1967, reflects a powerful convergence of these presences: the words are those of Du Bois; the first page of the orchestral version states that it is "in memory of Abbie Mitchell and Langston Hughes" (see Figure 3.1); and the second part of the work is subtitled *Darkwater*, suggesting that she was using the autobiography *Darkwater* itself as the source for her text.[11] The ideas whose course began with Du Bois's own maturity in the 1890s had run their course throughout his career and finally, some seventy years later, found musical fruit in the creative imagination of Margaret Bonds.

From Du Bois to Bonds: The *Credo* in Words and Tones

A synoptic overview of W. E. B. Du Bois's *Credo* and its basic relationship to Margaret Bonds's setting reveals the importance of the rift between Du Bois and Washington in shaping the specific

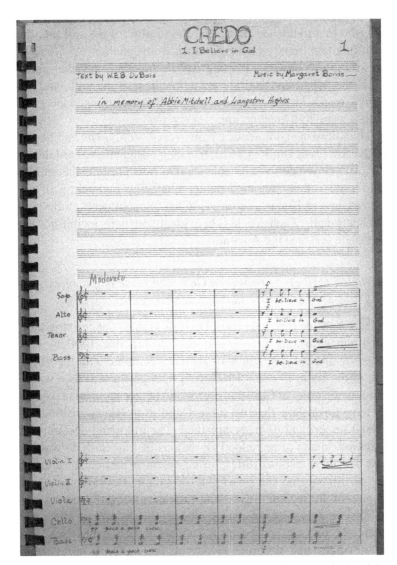

Figure 3.1 First page of the score of *Credo*. Booth Family Center for Special Collections, Georgetown University Libraries, Washington, DC, shelfmark GTM-130530, Box 18, folder 5. Used by permission.

ideas, the enduring currency of his words nearly seven decades after he first published them, and the fertility of the soil that the resulting text found in Bonds's musical imagination. As we shall see, these two creeds – the one verbal, the other musical – draw upon the potent and entirely apt symbolism of the arch, and Du Bois's words also resonated with the Black feminist aspects of Bonds's creative imagination.

The following commentary is an overview only. The numbering of the articles of Du Bois's text, like their designation as articles, is editorial, provided for convenience (Du Bois presents the articles as a series of unnumbered paragraphs). The numbering of the movements of Bonds's setting is given in parentheses, following the autographs. Each article is here identified by its incipit; for the complete text, see the Appendix.

Article I (No. 1): "I believe in God, who made of one blood all nations that on earth do dwell."

As we shall see (pp. 106–109), Du Bois granted special structural importance to this article and the closing one (Article IX). Rhetorically, the first words of Article I combine with the titular use of the Latin *Credo* ("I believe") to align the text as a whole with a wide array of Christian creeds and other canonical texts, and thereby to declare that its subject and professions are both of sacred import and divinely ordained. The following declarations that God "made of one blood all nations that on earth do dwell," and that these nations differ "in no essential particular" and are "alike in soul and the possibility of infinite development," are important in several ways. The article as a whole denies the validity of the reigning theses of scientific racism in the early twentieth century: polygenism (which argued that Black and White races had different origins and ancestors), polygenetic evolution (which applied polygenism to evolutionary theories both before Darwin and after), and the Hamitic hypothesis, which divided the African origins of the races into Saharan ("Hamitic") versus sub-Saharan groups and proposed that most or all innovation in the latter was the result of infiltration, immigration, or importation into "negroid" races. The article also disputes the assertion of contemporary scientific racism that, because of their supposedly separate origins and this (specious) history, "negroid" races had limited potential for knowledge, understanding, innovation, and progress.

More particularly, the 1920 version of this article differs from its 1904 counterpart in two significant ways. The 1920 formulation "made of one blood all *nations*" was a revision of the 1904 version's "made of one blood all *races*" (emphases added) – probably reflecting both Du Bois's evolving concept of race and the fact that the 1920 version was written after the end of World War I, a global trauma that widely changed understandings of the meanings of nation, race, and ethnicity. Moreover, the original text declared that God made of one blood "all men, black and white," but the 1920 revision changed the latter phrase to "black *and brown* and white" (emphasis added). This change more emphatically disputes the Hamitic hypothesis, but it is also significant because it reflects Du Bois's increasing awareness that what he had in 1903 (in *The Souls of Black Folk*) termed "the color line" was better described as "the *world* color line," including all of what he generally termed "the darker races" – especially those of the Indian subcontinent.[12]

Like Du Bois, Bonds grants special structural significance to this movement. She sets the first article as a powerful chorus in A minor (*moderato*, 52 mm.), one whose opening declaration "I believe in God" erupts from a gradual *crescendo* on *A* as a communal declaration (Ex. 3.1). The initial declaration is striking because it is cast entirely in parallel fifths and octaves and uses G natural rather than the G sharp that one might expect: these features belong to the stylistic lexicon commonly used to suggest primal and "folk" styles – entirely fitting for an orchestral choral work that challenged the predominantly White, "cultured" norms of concert music. At "I believe that all men, black and brown and white, are brothers," the tone softens as the key turns to A major and the voices enter one after another. "Differing in no essential particular" is set in G major (activating the already-heard natural seventh, *G*, at a structural level), and the music swerves back into A minor in order to associate "and alike in soul [etc.]" with the divine provenance of the initial

Example 3.1 *Credo*: "I Believe in God," mm. 1–13.

profession of faith in God and the sacrality of the ideas expressed in the *Credo* as a whole. The movement closes in the tonic but inconclusively, with a protracted *diminuendo* on open fifths as the choir declares "I believe" and the accompaniment reiterates the dactylic rhythm of that declaration in diminution.

Article II (No. 2): "Especially do I believe in the Negro Race."

This article specifically focuses on Black folk. The attributes that Du Bois ascribes to "the Negro Race" ("the beauty of its genius, the sweetness of its soul, and its strength in that meekness") reflect his early belief that nations were rooted in "race spirits," as well as his conviction, forcefully articulated already in an 1897 speech to the American Negro Academy, that Blacks had too long been taught "certain assumptions as to [their] natural abilities, as to [their] political, intellectual and moral status, which [they] felt were wrong," and that aside from these "certain assumptions" they had "been led to deprecate and minimize race distinctions."[13]

These were widespread nineteenth-century assumptions, a part of Du Bois's upbringing, ideas that were still current in the philosophy, politics, and science of the late nineteenth and early twentieth centuries. But while Article II reflects Du Bois's continued subscription to those now-discredited notions – indeed, the "one blood" clause of Article I reverses his position in the 1897 speech – the fact that the attributes he ascribes to "the Negro Race" are unanimously affirmative and have nothing to do with skin color reflects his solicitation to Blacks to affirm their own inherent humanity, both because of and separate from the skin colors that made African diasporic folk the subject of prejudice and discrimination by non-Blacks. Most importantly, having critically reviewed prevalent contemporary views on Blackness, accepted what was acceptable and rejected what was not, and added his own wisdom that was largely absent from contemporary racial discourse, Du Bois alluded to the third Beatitude (Matthew 5:5) to submit a vitally important prediction – the most overt in the entire *Credo* – that the attributes personified by Black folk "shall yet inherit this turbulent earth."

Out of these pronouncements both traditional and modern, critical and affirmative, Bonds creates a memorable movement for soprano and chorus in *A* mixolydian, with gapped scales and particular emphasis on the fifth and sixth scale degrees. These traits are characteristic of vernacular repertoires generally, and in the context of a movement whose text celebrates "the Negro Race" they clearly affirm Black vernacular styles specifically. Moreover, the form and structure of No. 2 are determined by the principle of call and response – a central element of African American music, and indeed of the worship experience in African American churches. After a brief introduction (mm. 53–56), the solo soprano leads (mm. 57–74; see Ex. 3.2) and then has its ideas taken up by the choir (mm. 75–101), with the soloist punctuating important ideas and phrases in the latter section, without interrupting the flow of the choir's declamation. And, finally, the whole is modeled

The Text and Music of the *Credo*

Example 3.2 *Credo*: "Especially Do I Believe in the Negro Race," mm. 56–72.

on the genre of the gospel song, which Langston Hughes described as "the offshoot of the spiritual" that was "perhaps the last refuge of . . . uncontaminated negro folk music."[14] In casting Du Bois's creed in the model of a gospel song – an intimately communal experience affirming Blackness – Bonds added another dimension to the affirmation and celebration of Black existence that underlay Article II of Du Bois's creed, affirming the music and the communal, participatory aesthetic of Black cultural life.

Article III (No. 3, mm. 102–39): "I believe in Pride of race and lineage and self."

This article confronts legal obstacles to racial equality in private life, chiefly familial and interpersonal relationships. Most generally, it challenges the philosophical, religious, and scientific worldview, ingrained in Whites from earliest childhood and forced upon persons of color, that dark skin was to be ashamed of, the mark of a lesser race and lineage. More specifically, "in pride of lineage so great as to despise no man's father" challenges the "racial purity" protocols that were built into the Black Codes that proliferated after Reconstruction and were codified into state laws in the South in the twentieth century.[15] "In pride of race so chivalrous as neither to offer bastardy to the weak" denounces White men who impregnated Black women but assumed little or no parental responsibility, casting a social stigma on the mothers and rendering children illegitimate. "Nor beg wedlock of the strong" refers to societal prescriptions on interracial marriage – the so-called "anti-miscegenation" laws that proliferated in the United States after Reconstruction. The final clause ("knowing that men may be brothers in Christ, even though they be not brothers-in-law") affirms that laws that forbid interracial bonds run contrary to God's law as represented in the teachings of Jesus of Nazareth and therefore must yield to the latter's authority.

Bonds musically combines this article with Article IV. After the glowing affirmation of No. 2, her music for Article III emphasizes the stern, negative tone of the latter, with a bracing cadence from the lushly scored A-major *largo* of the foregoing movement to a spartan D minor, *declamando*, for *divisi* male chorus with

Example 3.3 *Credo*: "I Believe in Pride of Race," mm. 102–109.

accompaniment (Ex. 3.3). The music turns to an agitated C minor at "knowing that men may be brothers in Christ" before pausing on a dominant-seventh of D minor,[16] with a *diminuendo* and *ritardando* that musically symbolizes the dissonance between antimiscegenation laws and Christ's law and leads directly to the next article.

Article IV (No. 3, mm. 140–83): "I believe in Service."

In his searing 1913 essay "The Church and the Negro," Du Bois distinguished between "menial service" and "Service" (uppercase *s*):

Why then are [Christ's] so-called followers deaf, dumb, and blind on the Negro problem – on the human problem?

Because they think they have discovered bypaths to righteousness which do not lead to brotherhood with the poor, the dirty, the ignorant and the black. "Make them servants," they say; "we need cooks." But can a whole race be doomed to menial service in a civilization where menial service is itself doomed? And when menial service has become Service and lost its social stigma, so that white folk want to enter such service, will they welcome black folk as fellow servants? Certainly not, and the slavery argument of this cry stands revealed.[17]

This Service, differentiated from menial service, is the subject of Article IV: not servitude born of subjugation to reinforce caste, but Service rooted in humility, respect, and honor for doing good for others regardless of race or caste. The clause "Wage is the 'Well done!' of the Master, who summoned all them that labor and are heavy laden, making no distinction between the black, sweating cotton hands of Georgia and the first families of Virginia" denotes the equality of all races and castes in the eyes of God, and "from the blackening of boots to the whitening of souls" evokes the color line even as it asserts the salutary effects of Service. The final phrase, "since all distinction not based on deed is devilish and not divine," reinforces these points as well as providing an important through line to Article V.

Bonds's music for this article is a continuation of that for the previous article, likewise scored for male voices only with accompaniment. Although the movement ends in D minor and is prepared by the half-cadence at the end of the previous article, it begins off-tonic and its harmonic language is pervasively unstable, yet calm (see Ex. 3.4). As the movement ends, Bonds's forceful declaration that "all distinction not based on deed is devilish and not divine" brings D minor – the key of the following article and movement – into focus via quartal harmonies.

Article V (No. 4): "I believe in the Devil and his angels."

This article, located at the exact midpoint of the text, is the affective nadir of the *Credo*. Accordingly, it focuses on the "devilish" antipodes of the "divine" values that inspire belief. To enumerate all these oppositions would have taken too much space, but Du Bois singles out for distinction opportunity, egalitarian interpersonal relationships, affirmative confidence in Blackness, and the beauty of "the image which their Maker stamped on a brother's soul."

Example 3.4 *Credo*: "I Believe in Service," mm. 147–53.

After the beautiful complexity of Bond's setting of Article IV, this article presents a musical image of "the Devil and his angels." It is scored as a resolute march for five-part chorus in mostly diminished-seventh chords, with an insistent drone, drumbeat, and interrupted tremolo in the lower registers of the accompaniment (Ex. 3.5).

Article VI (No. 5): "I believe in the Prince of Peace. I believe that War is Murder."

The first sentence of this article establishes a connection to the God and "Maker" already mentioned by using the phrase "the Prince of Peace" to invoke Jesus of Nazareth. But the word *peace* itself becomes the springboard for the remainder of the article,

Example 3.5 *Credo*: "I Believe in the Devil and His Angels," mm. 188–96.

which condemns war, imperialist expansionism, and capitalist exploitation in the strongest possible terms and foretells that the present-day strength of those forces of "the Devil and his angels" will inevitably be vanquished by those allied with the Prince of Peace. The article as a whole recapitulates Du Bois's frequent and strenuous opposition to the Berlin Conference of 1884–85, where the major European powers formalized and negotiated their own territorial and commercial claims in Africa with no participation or representation from the African peoples themselves,[18] and it anticipates Du Bois's perspectives on Japan and China in World War II and Maoist China,[19] as well as his 1953 prediction[20] that a future crisis of world capitalism would eventually prompt peoples of color worldwide to unite in a broadly socialist society.

Structurally, this article's positive/negative polarity (a seven-word topic sentence invoking peace followed by forty-seven words about war, capitalist oppression, and exploitation) is significant because the first sentence provides continuity with the affirmative spirit of the *Credo* as a whole, while the balance of the article maintains a strong through line from the subtly ambivalent complexities of Article IV and the stern condemnations of Article V.[21] More importantly, this article concurs with the 1920 revision of Article I in emphasizing that the color line was a *world*, not national, problem, and in suggesting that a future unity of "weaker and darker nations" was the eventual cure for the manifestly evil contemporary situations whereby a global minority of White nations ruled over and profited from the subjugation of "the millions of black men in Africa, America, and the Islands of the Sea, not to speak of the brown and yellow myriads elsewhere" (as Du Bois had put it in his address to the Pan-African Conference in London in 1900).[22]

The structural and exegetical importance of this article is underscored by Du Bois's construal of *peace* in the phrase "I believe in the Prince of Peace." Here, *peace* denotes not merely the absence of violence or conventional warfare and not merely what Phil Hopkins has termed "the glittering generality of good-will towards men,"[23] but rather a universal humanism fostered by global equality and freedom from oppression.[24] Viewed this way, Du Bois's decision to begin an article decrying war and colonialist oppression with a declaration of belief in peace is not a disconnect, as one might initially suspect, but rather a simple thesis statement, to wit: *I believe in global equality that rejects war and oppression as forces that will and must eventually corrupt and decay.* The declaration of belief in peace thus continues rather than disrupts the through line of Articles IV–VI. Accordingly, Bonds's setting of this article is the most affectively and stylistically complex in the entire work. She offers a significant departure from Du Bois's text by presenting this article in *da capo* form (Figure 3.2). The opening section is a marked departure from the "devil music" of No. 4, a serene and lushly scored and harmonized F-major setting, *andante*, of "I believe in the Prince of Peace" for women's chorus with support, in the orchestral version, from strings and woodwinds (mm. 219–35; see Ex. 3.6a). The remainder of the article, condemning war and capitalist exploitation of "weaker and darker nations," abruptly turns to D minor, the key of "the devil and his angels" in No. 4, and becomes increasingly turbulent (mm. 236–54; Ex. 3.6b). This is then followed by an expanded reprise of the *A* section (mm. 255–88), still led by the women's voices but with the men's voices responding and echoing. But arguably the most telling aspect of the movement is that Bonds musically interprets the eventual victory of the poor, the oppressed, and the darker peoples as a great climax in C major (mm. 244–53). This tonality of this climax in turn serves as the dominant of the return to F major for the reprise of "peace" of the *A* section. The vividness of the symbolism is extraordinary: the death of wicked strength born of the Devil and his angels leads directly to peace and the Prince of Peace.

Text	I believe in the Prince of Peace.	I believe that War is murder [etc.]. . .	I believe in the Prince of Peace.
Vocal Scoring	SSA	SATB	SATB
Key	F	d → unstable → C	F
Mm.	215–35	236–54	255–88

Figure 3.2 *Credo*: Structure of No. 5.

93

Example 3.6 *Credo*: "I Believe in the Prince of Peace," (a) mm. 218–23; (b) mm. 236–39; (c) climax at "the death of that strength," mm. 244–53.

Example 3.6 (cont.)

Article VII (No. 6, mm. 289–354 and passim): "I believe
in Liberty for all men."

After the sharp and negative tone of Articles III–VI, Article VII
returns to the positive outlook of Article II. Its reference to "all
men" continues the previous articles' affirmative solicitations
toward global equality. "The space to stretch their arms and their
souls" alludes to Article I's themes of opportunity and "the possibility of infinite development," while "the right to vote" is a direct
reference to the disfranchisement of Black folk in the United
States. "The right to breathe" – a phrase endowed with renewed
horror worldwide in the years 2020–21, after the murder of George
Floyd by a Minneapolis police officer – probably is a direct reference to the rising tide of lynchings of Blacks that were sweeping
the United States at the time the *Credo* was written (since the
medical cause of death in lynchings usually is respiratory
asphyxia). And finally, "enjoy the sunshine" probably refers to
the fact that Blacks in the segregated sharecropping South were
forced to work in the fields on every fair day and thus rarely able to
"enjoy" the sunshine.

Bonds, in keeping with the generally positive tone of both
Articles VII and VIII, combines the two into a single movement
(No. 6) spanning a total of 116 measures. The movement is scored
for bass-baritone soloist with chorus and accompaniment and cast
in a radiant D major, with emphasis on the fifth and sixth scale
degrees.[25] This counterbalances the *Credo*'s other movement for
soloist with chorus (No. 2), yet the length and the key of No. 6
grant it special significance in the *Credo* as a whole (see discussion
below, pp. 107–10). The movement's open voicing and widely
spaced chords evoke "the space to stretch their arms and their
souls" spoken of in the text, and indeed Bonds musically depicts
that stretching itself, as the bass-baritone solo moves progres-
sively higher, from *C sharp¹* to *D sharp¹* and then to a long
E sharp¹ on "the right to breathe and the right to vote, the freedom
to choose their friends, enjoy the sunshine" (see Ex. 3.7). But
because these rights are still, for Black folk, things of the future,
the cry for them ends only deceptively, with the dominant-seventh
chord on *C sharp* in mm. 309–12 moving not to *F sharp* (minor or

Example 3.7 *Credo*: "I Believe in Liberty for All Men," mm. 300–13.

major), as one would expect, but to an A^{11} chord that finally turns indirectly to D major in mm. 316–18.

Article VIII (No. 6, mm. 355–404): "I believe in the Training of Children, black even as white."

This article's emphasis on the training of children connects it to the references to "opportunity" in Article I and Article IV, and its reference to "some large vision of beauty and goodness and truth" connects to Article VII. Equally important, the phrase "not for pelf or peace, but for life lit by some large vision of beauty and goodness and truth" is striking because it rejects the widespread popular view of nature as middle-class playground and portrays it instead as the locus of the individual's connection to the God (of beauty, goodness, and truth) who is the source of the sacred charge of the *Credo* as a whole.[26] Du Bois's invocation of biblical (Old Testament) imagery with the phrase "the leading out of little souls into the green pastures and beside the still waters" (cf. Psalm 23:2: "He maketh me to lie down in green pastures: he leadeth me beside the still waters," *King James Version*) underscores that the *Credo*'s mission of racial justice and global equality is one that emanates from God himself.

As mentioned above, Bonds combines this article with Article VII, treating it as the second portion of No. 6. In fact, it emerges as even more important than the first part of that movement. Bonds marks its tempo "Little faster," and its overall form may be described as call and response. The bass-baritone soloist leads in mm. 355–74, the chorus dominates thereafter, and the soloist leads the choral texture for the remainder of the movement. Additionally, as shown in Ex. 3.8a–c, Bonds uses the material from the "thinking, dreaming, working as they will" section first stated in mm. 323–27 and 339–45 of Article VII as a kind of ritornello, bringing it back at the end of Article VIII (mm. 388–94) in some of the most sumptuously beautiful choral writing of the entire twentieth-century repertoire.

Most tellingly, where Du Bois provides a measure of closure at the end of the article (via the period at the end of "like Esau, for mere meat barter their birthright in a mighty nation"), Bonds does not. Instead, the sonority at the cadence in "a mighty nation" is a ninth chord, with the soloist proclaiming a sustained *E* in the middle of the D-major cadential close (Ex. 3.9). From here, the chorus once more repeats "I believe in Liberty" – softly, and ending on a major-seventh chord, with a *C sharp* in the *divisi* sopranos: resolution of the article's desiderata is once again denied.

Example 3.8 *Credo*: "I Believe in Liberty for All Men," (a) mm. 321–36; (b) mm. 339–41; (c) 388–98.

Example 3.8 (cont.)

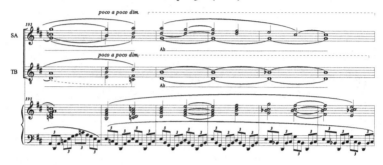

Example 3.9 *Credo*: "I Believe in Liberty for All Men," mm. 381–84.

Article IX (No. 7): "I believe in patience ... Patience with God!"

Du Bois's *Credo* ends with a return to the opening invocation of God and portrayal of the sacrality of the quest for justice and global equality. This sacrality reminds that the quest for global equality emanates from God himself, that those engaged in this pursuit are acting on a divine mandate, and that – in forceful contradiction to the ideas of Booker T. Washington and his followers – "the darker races" of the world color line did not need to earn equality or prove themselves worthy of political power, civil rights, and high-quality education. "Patience," therefore, denotes not calm and uncomplaining endurance, but rather *perseverance* – "constancy or diligence in work, exertion, or effort" (*OED Online*).

In this context, "patience with the weakness of the Weak" admonishes that those who for centuries have been taught that they are inferior, taught to cringe, taught to endure without complaint should persevere and not give up. "Patience with . . . the strength of the Strong" admonishes not to expect the powerful to share their power willingly or soon, but to persevere in the quest for justice despite their intransigence. "Patience . . . with the prejudice of the ignorant" solicits perseverance despite the ignorance of racist prejudice, and "patience with . . . the ignorance of the Blind" admonishes to persist even though some cannot see past their ignorant prejudice. Finally, "patience with the tardy triumph of Joy and the mad chastening of Sorrow" reminds that the intractable travails, injustices, and inequalities of the racist and exploitive present will, with our work and God's decree, pass.

Bonds sets this closing moment in Du Bois's archlike structure as a logical continuation of the first, and its fulfillment. Like the first movement, it is in A minor, and it uses essentially the same thematic material – except that while No. 1 fades out without a definitive conclusion, No. 7 begins as an almost literal quotation but then musically drives toward "the tardy triumph of Joy and the mad chastening of Sorrow," creating a powerful climax out of these words both tragic and redemptive (Ex. 3.10). Moreover, No. 7 quotes from and alludes to the intervening five movements – so that this last movement is not just the completion of the first but also, equally importantly, a summation of all that has come before. The power of that goal is vividly depicted in the final bars, as the accompaniment, after a cadence from E-flat major to A, with prominent F-major sonorities, reiterates the dactylic "I believe" motive beneath the chorus's sustained proclamation of "God" on open fifths and octaves: the triumph of justice will be attained only with mighty effort and is still a thing of the future, but it is a thing of God, divinely assured.

This synopsis gives some idea not only of the general layout of the Du Bois and Bonds *Credo*s, but also of the exegetical richness

The Text and Music of the *Credo*

Example 3.10 *Credo*: "I Believe in Patience," mm. 434–56.

Example 3.10 (cont.)

of both. This richness, however, also opens the door for further
interpretive insights that connect Du Bois's and Bonds's *Credo*s to
each other, to *The Montgomery Variations*, and to the context of
the great social-justice movements of the twentieth century. Those
insights are the subject of the remainder of this chapter.

Practical and Interpretive Issues

Perhaps the most obvious issue facing anyone who wants to come
to terms with Du Bois's text and Bonds's setting of it is that of
genre. Du Bois's *Credo* is obviously a creed, though it also has

attributes of a manifesto and is sometimes described as a prose-poem. Bonds's *Credo*, for its part, is sometimes described as a cantata. While the work may be fairly viewed as a nonnarrative multi-movement composition for soloists, chorus, and piano or orchestra, and thus generally consistent with the J. S. Bach cantatas that Bonds would have known, that designation tends to obscure Bonds's own articulated views concerning its overall form – for Bonds's letters refer to it as "Credo and Darkwater" or "Darkwater and Credo," and the autograph title label on the cover of the autograph full score labels it "CREDO and DARKWATER / text by W.E.B. Du Bois / music by Margaret Bonds / for Chorus and Orchestra."[27] Moreover, in both the piano–vocal score and the full score, the beginning of No. 5 is preceded by the uppercase indication "DARKWATER." This does not mean that Bonds viewed the work as two separate compositions, for the binding and title page of the piano–vocal score label it simply "CREDO," as do the first pages of the piano–vocal score and the full score themselves, and the autograph pagination runs continuously throughout the entire work in both manuscripts. But it does mean that a major structural break between Nos. 4 and 5 was integral to Bonds's own conception of the work – and this overall bipartite organization is not conveyed by the generally unilinear term *cantata*.

But setting Du Bois's creed to music also posed other practical challenges laced with structural and interpretive implications. Most basic among these are the sheer quantity of words and the fact that Du Bois's *Credo* is prose, not poetry. It takes longer to sing words than to speak or read them, and the text of Du Bois's *Credo* runs to five hundred and five words (this is 46 percent longer than the text of J. S. Bach's Cantata 140, which runs to about twenty-six minutes in brisk tempo). This alone might have threatened to make Bonds's setting overlong, even without any textual repetitions or instrumental passages without voices. Moreover, prose, because of its lack of regular meters, rhyme, and cadence, is difficult to set to music predicated (as Bonds's is) on the cadentially articulated, metrically periodic phrase. The challenge is not unprecedented, of course, but traditionally composers have introduced verbal and/or musical repetition in order to compensate for the problem – and this would exacerbate the challenge of length/duration.

Moreover, Bonds, for evidently interpretive reasons,[28] did introduce four structurally significant musical reiterations of portions of Du Bois's text. The simplest of these occur in No. 2, where she reiterates the entire text; and Nos. 3 and 6, which combine Articles III–IV and VII–VIII. The third, more complicated handling obtains in No. 5, where Bonds treated Du Bois's unilinear text as a *da capo* form in which the "Prince of Peace" serves as the *A* section and the remainder of the article serves as the *B* section – a reinterpretation that affects both the sequence of ideas and the proportions of the two significantly contrasting areas of the text. As shown in Figure 3.2 (p. 93), in Du Bois's text, forty of this article's forty-seven words (85 percent) are devoted to the "war is murder" proposition, but in Bonds's setting, the "war" section of Article VI comprises only nineteen bars (about 23 percent), while the framing "Prince of Peace" sections (mm. 215–35 and 255–88) comprise sixty-five bars (about 77 percent).

Bonds's structural reinterpretation of Article VI leads to her fourth structural reinterpretation, which is deeply personal: in creating the reprise of "The Prince of Peace" in No. 5, Bonds placed the theme of peace directly adjoining the theme of "liberty for all men" and "the Training of little children"[29] in No. 6 (Article VII). This was a poetic vision that effectively combined Articles VI, VII, and VIII into a single meta-article unified by the "thinking, dreaming" ritornello, suggesting that liberty is not merely the affective opposite of war and racist, capitalist exploitation, but an extension or outgrowth of peace. Indeed, Bonds's music suggests that, for her, No. 6 is the telos of the entire *Credo*. Like No. 3, No. 6 combines two articles of Du Bois's text, and indeed, No. 6 is the only movement that stays in the major mode throughout. At 116 measures, it is also by far the longest movement. Its key is the parallel major of that of No. 3 – an apt bit of tonal symbolism, in that No. 3 is a plea to reconcile the disparities between the Black and White conditions and No. 6 is about the *equality* of Black and White: "all men," "children, black even as white," "uncursed by color . . . in the kingdom of beauty and love."

Most important, though, is that Du Bois and Bonds both organize their *Credo* in a form derived from the principles of the arch – an artfully symbolic structure. In architecture, painting, poetry, and literature, the vertical arch is a potent symbol for many things that are germane to the *Credo*. Arches symbolize the passage from one area (here, the injustice of the present) to another (freedom, justice, and global equality in the future). Reaching upward and drawing the observer's eye skyward, they also epitomize aspirational strength born of collective and mutual support, since their basic principle is the downward transference of weight through contingent, mutually supporting elements (the divine mandate for racial justice and global equality, the transference of that mandate downward to humanity, and the spread of the thrust in that direction). Finally, although known in almost all cultures globally, arches originated in what Du Bois terms the "darker races" – a historical patent that would have appealed to Du Bois's assertions that contemporary Black and Brown folk needed to recognize the error of the White world's portrayal of itself as the great innovator of world history, and to take pride also in the long history of great Black contributions to history and culture.

Du Bois, ever fascinated with art and architecture, was certainly well aware of this symbolism and its historical manifestations. He declared that "[t]he Negro is primarily an artist,"[30] and throughout his career his social imagination expressed itself in visual as well as verbal terms; he used visual images and visual techniques to drive his points home to readers – often in sophisticated ways.[31] His writings on art, from the early "The Art and Art Galleries of Modern Europe" (1895–96) on,[32] make clear his constant concern that art possess authenticity, structural integrity ("unity of purpose"), abstract appeal, and topical applicability. In 1926 he suggested that because art revealed (through the acclaim afforded Countee Cullen, Langston Hughes, Jesse Redmon Fauset, Walter White, and others) that the color line was a fictitious construct enforced as reality, it – art – was "the real solution of the color problem." His dictum that "all art is propaganda" later in the same essay reflects, in the words of Eric J. Sundquist, his "deeply held belief in the ethical and political responsibility of art and literature."[33]

Given the interpretive and exegetic findings presented earlier in this chapter, it seems fitting to describe the archlike form of Du Bois's text and Bonds's setting thereof as *the divinely mandated arch of social justice* (see Figure 3.3). The key to understanding this organizational expression is the text's verbiage and its parallels and groupings in subject and character: the word *God* is mentioned only in the first and last articles, imparting an obvious symmetry to those two articles and establishing them as the springers, the supports or imposts at the outer ends of an arch, which anchor the whole, and from which the remaining elements "spring." Articles II–III and VII–VIII, as noted above, are strongly affirmative in tone: they uplift Black humanity, the equality of all races, liberty, and education, and they attach to the springers' proclamation of belief in God to cast that uplift as something that is divinely mandated. The parallel character and tone of these articles makes them the internal voussoirs of the arch, setting and executing the curve of the structure's main body. And Articles IV–VI, which exhibit a sterner, more negative character, collectively constitute the keystone, the summit that locks the whole together. Because of the connections between this keystone, the surrounding voussoirs, and the springers, the *Credo* as a text, despite its length and its topical variety, possesses the unity and structural integrity that is necessary for any vertical arch to withstand the forces that challenge it.

The elements of Bonds's archlike structure (shown in the lower portion of Figure 3.3) are distributed differently than those of Du Bois's, but the parallel design of the two is unmistakable. The key, mode, and scoring of the outermost movements (Nos. 1 and 7) reveal those movements to be springers, as in Du Bois's text. No. 2 ("Especially do I believe in the Negro Race") serves as the first internal voussoir and sets the curve of the arc toward racial justice. Nos. 3, 4, and 5 (Articles III–VI), the keystone, condemn war and capitalist exploitation and then provide an extended reprise of the music of peace from the beginning of No. 5, teaching through music that the demise of exploitation and oppression depicted in mm. 244–53 of that movement (see Ex. 3.6c, above) brings

	I	II	III	IV	V	VI	VII	VIII	IX
	[springer]		[voussoirs]			[keystone]		[voussoirs]	[springer]
Du Bois (1904/1920) Article	I	II	III	IV	V	VI	VII	VIII	IX
Key	God – all races made of one blood	Especially do I believe in the Negro race	I believe in Pride of race and lineage and self	I believe in Service ...making no distinction ...since all distinction not based on deed is devilish and not divine	I believe in the Devil and his angels, who wantonly work to narrow the opportunity of struggling human beings ...	I believe in the Prince of Peace. I believe that War is Murder. ... the wicked conquest of weaker and darker nations by nations whiter and stronger but foreshadows the death of that strength	I believe in Liberty for all men ... uncursed by color	I believe in the Training of Children, black even as white	Patience with God
Theme	*Divine imperative for racial justice*	*Humanity of Blackness, equality of races in the eyes of God*		*[Justice as cure for oppression]*			*Equality of freedom and opportunity regardless of race = justice*		*Inevitable victory of divine imperative for racial justice*
Bonds (1965–67) No.	1	2	3 (III+IV)		4 (V)	5 (VI)	6 (VII + VIII)		7
Scoring	Chorus	A solo w/ chorus	Chorus		Chorus	Chorus	Bar. solo w/ chorus		Chorus
Key	a-A-G-(a)	A	d		d	F-d-C-F	D		a-A-G-C-(a)
Mm.	1–52	53–101	102–183		184–214	215–88	289–404		405–455
Length	52	49	82		31	73	116		51
	[springer]	[voussoir]		[keystone]			[voussoir]		[springer]

Figure 3.3 *Credo*: Archlike structure of Du Bois's text and Bonds's music.

peace and justice. No. 6, the second voussoir, serves as the telos or goal of the directional arc toward racial justice, positioned to portray liberty for all as the consequent of peace. And with this arc completed, Bonds returns to a movement for full chorus in the tonic A minor, musically soliciting us not to waver in our trust that "the weakness of the weak and the strength of the strong, the prejudice of the Ignorant and the ignorance of the Blind" are but moments within an arc toward racial justice that is mandated by God himself.

Conclusions: From "The Damnation of Women" to Bonds's *Credo*

As discussed in the Introduction, relational issues and their attendant creative, personal, and professional outlooks were central to Bonds's conception of herself and her work, so much so that we cannot understand the *Credo* without coming to terms with them. They account for the decision – by a Black woman who even in the 1960s was still expected to prioritize familial duties, compose in smaller forms rather than public ones, and (as she put it in the 1964 interview) "keep apologizing for" her talent[34] – to set a text by a Black man as a multi-movement composition for soloists, chorus, and (ultimately) orchestra. And because of them – because of the centrality of Bonds's self-identification as Woman and as a Black artist – Bonds's *Credo* is perhaps best understood as her personal manifesto, an artistic gambit that aspired to make good on the efforts Estella Bonds and other forebears had invested in her, and to put her God-given gifts to use in the struggle for equality for "our oppressed Race."[35]

Crucial in this regard are the similarities and differences between Bonds's Black feminism and Du Bois's thinking about Black women – for the *Credo* never once mentions women. Certainly Du Bois was a lifelong advocate for Black women.[36] He actively (and successfully) fought Monroe Trotter's opposition to women's inclusion in the Niagara Movement (see Chapter 4), and a number of his assertions advocating for women were bold and brilliant in their own historical moment – for example "all womanhood is hampered today because the world on which it is emerging is a world that tries to worship both virgins and mothers but in the end despises mother-hood and despoils virgins"; and "the uplift of women is, next to the problem of the color line and the peace movement, our greatest modern cause."[37] Indeed, Du Bois's perspective viewing "white and male supremacist capitalist societies [as] simultaneously race-, gender-, and class-specific and hegemonic," foreshadows intersectional approaches to Blackness and womanism.[38] But this advocacy did not translate into full-fledged espousal of equality of the sexes – for Du Bois's writings consistently portray the cause of racial justice as one in which women played vital roles as wives, mothers, and supportive activists but men, not women, were the intellectual and spiritual leaders.

To term Du Bois's outlook "feminist" or "pro-feminist" would be too strong (it would be starkly reactionary in the context of the second-wave feminism of the 1960s, when Bonds composed her *Credo*), and to term it "masculinist" would be too weak; Rabaka's term "male-womanist" is probably the fairest summary.[39] In any event, although Du Bois's writings that are contemporaneous with his *Credo* resonate with some of Bonds's views expressed in the "Destiny" letter and her other writings, we cannot deny that Du Bois's outlook, as reflected in the *Credo*, would have been at odds with Bonds's own. In fact, the *Credo*'s most overt reference to the complex of issues entailed in "the woman problem" is its admonition concerning "the education of Children" (Article VIII). The question thus becomes: If, as seems obvious, the centrality of Woman to Bonds's own outlook inevitably transferred into her own musical creed, how did she reconcile the contradictions between the male-womanist perspective of the text's author with her own views?

One important answer lies in her personal understanding of the very God invoked in Articles I and IX of the *Credo*. Certainly Du Bois, in keeping with tradition and with his own biases, viewed God as a masculine deity. But as shown in Chapter 2 (p. 51–52), Bonds's programs for *The Montgomery Variations* describe God as "the Mother-Father God" and "Father and Mother to all people." Although "Father" comes first in the latter description and Bonds goes on to use only the masculine possessive pronoun "His," her use of the descriptors "Mother-Father" and "Father and

Mother" for God shows that she viewed the source of the divinely mandated arc toward racial justice as being Woman as well as Man. That perspective also plays out and is further extended in No. 6, the second of the *Credo*'s two solo movements. Indeed, the second part of No. 6 (mm. 355–404) deals with the very complex of issues that Bonds faced as a Black woman: that of children and their education. The complexity of this is compounded by the fact that she was writing a large-scale choral–orchestral work on a difficult text by a male author – a compositional sphere that many others considered the prerogative of men. Bonds had not yet had children when she penned the deeply emotional 1942 letters discussed earlier in this book, for her daughter, Djane, would not be born until 1946. But Djane Richardson was grown by the time Bonds penned the *Credo*, and by that point Margaret Bonds had a full lifetime of motherhood, including her own upbringing in Estella Bonds's strong and devoted care, behind her.

It is thus probably not a coincidence that Article VIII of the Du Bois *Credo*, with its portrayal of the education of children as a key to "life lit by some large vision of beauty and goodness and truth . . . in a mighty nation," receives some of the setting's most extended and striking music – 116 bars in a radiant D major. Even more foundational to this movement than Bonds's own personal experience in motherhood raising Djane, however, is the generational perspective she set forth in her letter of December 17, 1942: the music of "I believe in the Training of little Children, black even as white," set apart from the foregoing material in tempo and texture, draws attention to the same sort of overarching generational progress, and to the idea that parents must work to enable their children to achieve their own *Destiny* – on their own terms and in order to achieve "life lit by some large vision of beauty and goodness and truth . . . in a mighty nation" (Du Bois) – that Bonds elaborates on in her "Destiny" letter: "[My mother] . . . is willing to die with nothing [so] that I shall fulfill my Destiny. . . . From my grandfather on down they all worked silently, quietly, in obscurity for Mankind, for our oppressed Race."[40] By following the "training of little children"[41] section with a return to the "thinking, dreaming, working as they will in the kingdom of beauty and love" passage, Bonds musically connects her setting of that text directly to her 1942 "Destiny" letter (see Ex. 3.8a–c, above). More important and direct than this, however, is that No. 2 (Article II) is the first moment within the divinely mandated arc toward racial justice. It is thus one of the most dramatically positioned, and thus rhetorically impactful, movements of the entire work. Its musical style reinforces this prominence. As shown in Figure 3.3 (p. 108), it directly follows a large chorus in the opposite mode, one in which the men's voices lead when the chorus is not declaiming homorhythmically. But the first movement ends inconclusively, yielding abruptly to the radiant, luxurious beauty of the work's crucial proclamation that "Especially do I believe in the Negro Race; in the beauty of its genius, the sweetness of its soul, and its strength in that meekness which shall yet inherit this turbulent earth." It is the only movement of Du Bois's text that begins with the word "especially," and the only movement in Bonds's setting that features a solo soprano. As a rhetorical gesture, then, No. 2 aptly parallels Bonds's rejection not just of the racial oppression so eloquently countered by Du Bois's texts, but also of the subservience that was still expected of women. Its rhetorical point is compelling: in the divinely mandated arc toward racial justice, *Black woman leads*.

But perhaps the most perceptive feature of Bonds's treatment of Du Bois's text derives from her settings of the outermost articles (the springers). Those two articles – the first phrase of Article I and the last phrase of Article IX – are the only instances of the word "God" in the text. In this sense, Du Bois's text is a closed cycle. But Bonds exploits the larger ramifications of that textual invocation of God's authority, reenvisioning the *Credo* as a musical cycle in which the material of the earlier movements, in keeping with well-established archetypes of cyclical form, is not closed, but carried further in the last movement, finally achieving its fulfillment there. Her setting of the last article begins by referencing that of the first article, but breaks free of its predecessor when "and alike in soul and the possibility of infinite development" would be expected. In No. 1, the music for those words alludes back to the "I believe in God" motive from mm. 1–13 but then dissolves. In No. 7 the energy abates momentarily at the reiteration of "I believe in Patience" at m. 437 but then quickly resurges, leading to a powerful climax on "the tardy triumph of Joy and the mad, mad, mad chastening of Sorrow" (see Ex. 3.10, pp. 102–103). The importance of this musical moment is underscored at two levels. Most obviously, the generally slow harmonic language of the *Credo* as a whole becomes complete stasis, shimmering with expectation, *pianissimo*, at Bonds's reiteration of "I believe in Patience" in mm. 436–37 – but Bonds breaks out of this stasis at the dramatic *crescendo* to "Joy" as the culmination of "patience with the tardy triumph of Joy."

That foreground-level harmonic motion has a counterpart at the background level. As shown in Figure 3.3, the first thirty-two bars of Bond's setting of Article IX are adapted from her setting of Article I. That material in the earlier article moves from the tonic A minor to G major before passing through C major to return abruptly to A minor. But in Article IX, *C* is not a passing harmony but rather the goal, one that is reinforced by its volume, scoring, duration, and move to its own subdominant (F major). This tonal sphere is the immediate locus of neither the bulk of the *Credo* nor (especially) the affective nadir in Articles III–V. Rather, it is the domain of the work's heart, No. 5 – which, as we have seen (p. 93), celebrates C major as the tonal symbol for the liberation of oppressed peoples everywhere, and F major as its tonal consequent, the domain of "the Prince of Peace." The C-major climax at "the tardy triumph of Joy" in No. 7 enacts the delayed tonal resolution of a structural dominant first set in motion in No. 1. Once this is achieved, the work's final bars combine the musical motive from "I believe in God" in the accompaniment with exclamations of "Patience with God" in the chorus, with chorus and accompaniment converging on the word "God," the chorus in six-part harmony and the sopranos sustaining a high A^2.

To interpret Du Bois's *Credo* as a grand cycle whose conclusion completes the ideas launched at the outset is to impart to the music an even greater and more dramatic sweep than that of the text. Moreover, the telos – or, by analogy to Bonds's own words – *destiny* of the ideas musical and other introduced in No. 1 is "the tardy triumph of Joy and the mad chastening of Sorrow." The dynamic emphasis on this climax, the expanded instrumentation vis-à-vis the analogous spot in No. 1, and the massive plagal emphasis on the word "joy" make clear that this triumph, while part of a future that must be awaited patiently, will be the fulfillment of what has come before – i.e., of the assertions made in the previous eight articles: the recognition that God made all nations of one blood, celebration of the negro race and its eventual inheritance, the right of all persons to liberty, and the imperative of equal education for all children in the interest of "life lit by some large vision of beauty and goodness and truth."

***

Du Bois's publication of his *Credo* was an inspired and courageous assertion that – contrary to the position of the White-dominated world of which his *Credo* was born – printed public declarations of faith, politics, and social justice were not the exclusive domain of White men. His audacity itself was in turn an inspiration to a world thirsty for such intrepid good will and vision, to the hundreds of thousands in the Great Migration who each year forsook the only land they and their forebears had ever known because (as Bonds would put it to Hughes in 1961) "they [*knew*] that God loves them *intensely*,"[42] that in turning their backs on the Jim Crow South they were pursuing the cause of a racial justice unknown to themselves or their ancestors – and doing so under a divine mandate. Margaret Bonds was among those heartened by his vision. But because of her pronounced sense of history, her conviction that she and her contemporaries had "a responsibility to [their] heritage," and her personal aspirations to "go farther" than those who had come before her, her own engagement with Du Bois's visionary creed does precisely that: it goes farther, and does so "for Mankind, for our oppressed Race."

These things – the relationships of Du Bois's and Bonds's respective creeds to their lineage, their refusal to submit to the limitations that their profoundly racist and sexist world would have imposed on them, their employment of powerfully symbolic structures, their topicality – are matters of poet's and composer's strategies for making of the *Credo* not just a statement of personal belief, but one that would offer a vision of courage and hope, inspiration and strength to their contemporaries. They are matters, all, of connections between text and context. The substance of those connections is the subject of Chapter 4.

Appendix:

Text of W. E. B. Du Bois, Credo

(from Darkwater: Voices from within the Veil) [New York: Harcourt, Brace & Howe, 1920], 3–4).

Credo

I BELIEVE in God, who made of one blood all nations that on earth do dwell. I believe that all men, black and brown and white, are brothers, varying through time and opportunity, in form and gift and feature, but differing in no essential particular, and alike in soul and the possibility of infinite development.

Especially do I believe in the Negro Race: in the beauty of its genius, the sweetness of its soul, and its strength in that meekness which shall yet inherit this turbulent earth.

I believe in Pride of race and lineage and self: in pride of self so deep as to scorn injustice to other selves; in pride of lineage so great as to despise no man's father; in pride of race so chivalrous as neither to offer bastardy to the weak nor beg wedlock of the strong, knowing that men may be brothers in Christ, even though they be not brothers-in-law.

I believe in Service – humble, reverent service, from the blackening of boots to the whitening of souls; for Work is Heaven, Idleness Hell, and Wage is the "Well done!" of the Master, who summoned all them that labor and are heavy laden, making no distinction between the black, sweating cotton hands of Georgia and the first families of Virginia, since all distinction not based on deed is devilish and not divine.

I believe in the Devil and his angels, who wantonly work to narrow the opportunity of struggling human beings, especially if they be black; who spit in the faces of the fallen, strike them that cannot strike again, believe the worst and work to prove it, hating the image which their Maker stamped on a brother's soul.

I believe in the Prince of Peace. I believe that War is Murder. I believe that armies and navies are at bottom the tinsel and braggadocio of oppression and wrong, and I believe that the wicked conquest of weaker and darker nations by nations whiter and stronger but foreshadows the death of that strength.

I believe in Liberty for all men: the space to stretch their arms and their souls, the right to breathe and the right to vote, the freedom to choose their friends, enjoy the sunshine, and ride on the railroads, uncursed by color; thinking, dreaming, working as they will in a kingdom of beauty and love.

I believe in the Training of Children, black even as white; the leading out of little souls into the green pastures and beside the still waters, not for pelf or peace, but for life lit by some large vision of beauty and goodness and truth; lest we forget, and the sons of the fathers, like Esau, for mere meat barter their birthright in a mighty nation.

Finally, I believe in Patience – patience with the weakness of the Weak and the strength of the Strong, the prejudice of the Ignorant and the ignorance of the Blind; patience with the tardy triumph of Joy and the mad chastening of Sorrow; – patience with God!

Notes

1. Harold Bloom, *The Anxiety of Influence: A Theory of Poetry* (New York: Oxford University Press, 1973); Sandra M. Gilbert and Susan Gubar, *The Madwoman in the Attic: The Woman Writer and the Nineteenth-Century Imagination* (New Haven, CT: Yale University Press, 1979).

2. Jeffrey Kallberg, "The Rhetoric of Genre: Chopin's Nocturne in G Minor," *Nineteenth-Century Music* 11 (1988): 238–61; rpt. and updated in his *Chopin at the Boundaries* (Cambridge, MA: Harvard University Press, 1996), 3–29.

3. See Du Bois's own "I am Resolved" (1912), published in *The Crisis* in 1912 (rept. in *W.E.B. Du Bois: Writings*, ed. Nathan Huggins [n.p.: Library of America, 1987], 1137–38) and his "Basic American Negro Creed," eventually published in his second auto-biography, *Dusk of Dawn* (1940); rept. in *W.E.B. Du Bois: Writings*, ed. Huggins, 788–89. The former, while not a creed per se, adopts the rhetoric and a form characteristic of creeds. The latter was written for the series of educational "Bronze Booklets" edited by Alain Locke and intended to provide a US national curriculum for Blacks' education. See Talmadge C. Guy and Stephen Brookfield, "W. E. B. Du Bois' Basic American Negro Creed and the Associates in Negro Folk Education: A Case of Repressive

Conclusions: From 'The Damnation of Women' to Bonds's *Credo*

Tolerance in the Censorship of Radical Black Discourse on Adult Education," *Adult Education Quarterly* 60 (2009): 65–76. Before these two documents of Du Bois (and the *Credo*), the most important previous similar document sole-authored by an African American was Frederick Douglass's "What the Black Man Wants," which had been published by the Massachusetts Anti-Slavery Society in 1865, and which Du Bois likely knew.

4. W. E. B. Du Bois, *Credo*, *The Independent* 57 (1904): 787.
5. W. E. B. Du Bois, *Dusk of Dawn*, in Huggins, *Du Bois: Writings*, 593.
6. The most concise summary of this position is found in Washington's so-called "Atlanta Compromise" speech, given at the Cotton States International Exposition on September 18, 1895.
7. David Levering Lewis, *W. E. B. Du Bois: Biography of a Race, 1868–1919* (New York: Henry Holt, 1993), 150–51, 229.
8. Quoted in Lewis, *Biography of a Race*, 175.
9. W. E. B. Du Bois, "Of Mr. Booker T. Washington and Others," in his *The Souls of Black Folk*, 2nd ed. (Chicago: A. C. McClurg & Co., 1903), 41–59 at 51.
10. See Robert Brown, "Introduction to 'The Social Significance of Booker T. Washington' by W. E. B. Du Bois," *Du Bois Review: Social Science Research on Race* 8 (2011): 359–66; the original text of Du Bois's essay is reproduced on pp. 367–76 of this issue. On the relationships between Du Bois and Washington, see especially Jacqueline M. Moore, *Booker T. Washington, W.E.B Du Bois, and the Struggle for Racial Uplift* (Wilmington, DE: Scholarly Resources, 2003); and chapter 10 ("Clashing Temperaments") in Lewis, *Biography of a Race*, 238–64.
11. The autograph full score for Bonds's setting of the Du Bois's *Credo* survives in the Booth Family Center for Special Collections in the Georgetown University Libraries, Washington, DC (shelfmark GTM-130530, Box 18, folder 5). The same center also holds a photocopy of the autograph piano–vocal score (shelfmark GTM-130530 Box 13, folder 1). Du Bois's *Credo* was available in myriad editions and formats by the time Bonds composed her setting in the mid-1960s, but only in Du Bois's *Darkwater* autobiography does "DARKWATER" appear as a running head just above the text of Article VI ("I believe in the Prince of Peace"). Bonds apparently mistook the running head as a new title for the last four articles of the text, rather than a running head that simply repeated the title of the book on left-hand pages in the volume. See W. E. B. Du Bois, *Darkwater: Voices from within the Veil* (New York: Harcourt, Brace and Howe, 1920).
12. See Bill V. Mullen, "W.E.B. Du Bois's Afro-Asian Fantasia," in his *Afro-Orientalism* (Minneapolis: University of Minnesota Press, 2004), 1–42.

13. Du Bois, "The Conservation of Races" (1897), in David Levering Lewis, *W.E.B. Du Bois: A Reader* (New York: Henry Holt, 1995), 20–27 at 20.

14. Langston Hughes, Remarks and readings at the San Francisco Museum of Art, December 5, 1958, at *The Poetry Center Digital Archive* https://diva.sfsu.edu/collections/poetrycenter/bundles/191214 (accessed May 10, 2021).

15. Still the best overview of these ideas, their historical origins, and their changing legal manifestations, in the United States is Cheryl Harris, "Whiteness as Property," *Harvard Law Review* 106 (1993): 1707–91.

16. In the original version for voices and piano, this sonority is a pure A-major chord, but in the final version with orchestra Bonds gave the tenors and basses the dyad *G-A*, creating a third-inversion seventh chord that musically emphasizes the dissonance of this legal conflict. Unfortunately, Rollo Dilworth's 2003 dissertation and the Dessoff Choirs' recent recording of the *Credo* based on it follow the rejected early reading and ignore Bonds's musically symbolic later revision.

17. W. E. B. Du Bois, "The Church and the Negro," in Phil Zuckerman, *Du Bois on Religion* (Walnut Creek, Cal.: AltaMira Press, 2000), 100.

18. See "The African Roots of the War" (1915), in Lewis, *Reader*, 642–51.

19. See especially Bill V. Mullen and Cathryn Watson, *W. E. B. Du Bois on Asia: Crossing the World Color Line* (Jackson: University Press of Mississippi, 2005).

20. W. E. B. Du Bois, "Negroes and the Crisis of Capitalism in the U.S.," *Monthly Review: An Independent Socialist Magazine* 4 (1953): 478–85; rept. *Monthly Review* 54 (2003): 36–43; and Lewis, *Reader*, 622–25.

21. I thank Professor Emeritus Phil Hopkins of Southwestern University for this important insight (personal communication of February 22, 2021).

22. Du Bois, "To the Nations of the World" (1900), quoted from Lewis, *Reader*, 639–41 at 639.

23. Personal communication of February 22, 2021.

24. This understanding of "peace" would later be championed, under Du Bois's influence, by Frantz Fanon (1925–61) in *Les damnés de la terre* (Paris: Maspero, 1961); Engl. as *The Wretched of the Earth*, trans. Constance Farrington (New York: Grove Press, 1963).

25. On the significance of this scoring in the context of other Black women composers' works that cast the baritone solo as a leader in the quest for justice, see Khyle Wooten's lecture "Religion, Resolve, and Rebuke: Dimensions of Justice in Baritone Solo Movements of Selected Choral Masterworks by Black Women Composers," delivered at the 25th anniversary conference of the African American Art Song Alliance (University of California–Irvine) on October 15, 2022 (www.youtube.com/watch?v=3fueRwmkbzY).

26. See John Claborn, *Civil Rights and the Environment in African-American Literature, 1895–1941* (London: Bloomsbury Academy, 2018), 55.
27. Georgetown University Bonds Papers, shelfmark GTM-130530, Box 18, folder 5.
28. See pp. 82–101.
29. The word *little* is not present in Du Bois's text; it was added by Bonds.
30. Du Bois, "Negro Art and Literature," quoted from Eric J. Sundquist, *The Oxford W.E.B. Du Bois Reader* (New York: Oxford University Press, 1996), 311.
31. The best-known (but also in some ways simplest) examples of this aspect of Du Bois's work are the celebrated visual data renderings in his exhibition catalog for the 1900 Paris World's Fair titled *The Negro in Georgia: A Social Study*; see Whitney Battle-Baptiste and Britt Rusert, *W.E.B. Du Bois's Data Portraits: Visualizing Black America: The Color Line at The Turn of the Twentieth Century* (Amherst, MA: The W.E.B. Du Bois Center at the University of Massachusetts–Amherst, 2018). See further Arnold Rampersad, *The Art and Imagination of W.E.B. Du Bois* (New York: Schocken Books, 1990), and Amy Helene Kirschke, *Art in Crisis: W.E.B. Du Bois and the Struggle for African American Identity and Memory* (Bloomington: Indiana University Press, 2007).
32. W. E. B. Du Bois, "The Art and Art Galleries of Modern Europe," in Herbert Aptheker,*Against Racism: Unpublished Essays, Papers, Addresses, 1887–1961, by W.E.B Du Bois* (Amherst: University of Massachusetts Press, 1985), 33–43.
33. Du Bois, "Criteria of Negro Art," quoted from Lewis, *Reader*, 512; David J. Sundquist, "Literature and Art," in *The Oxford W.E.B. Du Bois Reader* (New York: Oxford University Press, 1996), 304.
34. "Women are expected to be wives, mothers and do all the nasty things in the community (Oh, I do them), and if a woman is cursed with talent, too, then she keeps apologizing for it" (Christina Demaitre, "She Has a Musical Mission: Developing Racial Harmony; Heritage Motivates Composing Career," *The Washington Post* 87, no. 253 [August 14, 1964]: C2.
35. See the "Destiny" letter of December 17, 1942 (pp. 20–23).
36. See Reiland Rabaka, "'The Damnation of Women': Critique of Patriarchy, Contributions to Black Feminism, and Early Intersectionality," in his *Du Bois: A Critical Introduction* (Cambridge: Polity, 2021), 95–120; further, Gary L. Lemons, "W. E. B. Du Bois: 'The Leading Male Feminist of His Time' and 'Most Passionate Defender of Black Women,'" in his *Womanist Forefathers: Frederick Douglass and W. E. B. Du Bois* (Albany: State University of New York Press, 2009), 53–80. For

a representative sampling of Du Bois's writings on what Lemons (p. 80) terms "the complexity of black women's oppression," see Part V ("Women's Rights") in Lewis, *Reader*, 291–314.

37. Du Bois, *Darkwater*, 165, 181. Du Bois's other most important writings on "the woman question" include the poem "The Burden of Black Women" (1907), "The Black Mother" (1912), "Hail Columbia!" (1913), "Woman Suffrage" (1915), and "Sex and Racism" (1957); all are included in Lewis, *Reader*, 291–314.

38. Reiland Rabaka, "W.E.B. Du Bois and 'The Damnation of Women': An Essay on Africana Anti-Sexist Critical Social Theory," *Journal of African American Studies* 7, no. 2 (2003): 37–60 at 53.

39. Rabaka, "W.E.B. Du Bois and 'The Damnation of Women,'" 52.

40. Bonds to Richardson, December 17, 1942.

41. As noted above, "little" is Bonds's addition; Du Bois says simply "the training of Children."

42. Bonds (Nassau) to Hughes (New York), March 23, 1961 (Yale JWJ 26, Box 16, folder 375: no. 258). For discussion of this letter, see Chapter 1 (p. 26).

4

INTERPRETING THE *CREDO* IN CONTEXT

Introduction: The Inheritance

To overestimate W. E. B. Du Bois's and Margaret Bonds's sense of the importance of the ancestral heritage and the significance of tendering a new contribution to the long and rich inheritance of creeds, manifestos, and social platforms would be impossible – and in fact, Du Bois's *Credo* (and thus also Bonds's setting of that text) is both a creed and a manifesto. In general, the term *creed* denotes a communal confession of religious or sacralized belief, usually uttered or recited with the sense that it is binding upon members of that community. Du Bois's use of the Latin (or Italian) verb *credo* ("I believe") further associates his text (via the Nicene Creed and Apostles' Creed) with the Roman Catholic, Lutheran, Calvinist, and Anglican churches, as well as the African Methodist Episcopal (AME) Church.[1] And Bonds, a devout Baptist, not only had lifelong experience with the Apostles' Creed and the Nicene Creed but certainly also approached the genre from the perspective of the long and distinguished role it played in the history of Western music: she likely was acquainted with the *Credo* of Palestrina's Pope Marcellus Mass and that of Vivaldi (RV 591), of course – but the conspicuous symmetry of her own setting of the Du Bois *Credo* recalls the symmetry of the Credo of the so-called B-minor Mass (BWV 232) of J. S. Bach – suggesting that in it she aligned herself with the composer whom she called "the father of all in Music."[2]

But the *Credo*s of Du Bois and Bonds also have properties of manifestos and social or political platforms – genres that are functionally similar to creeds but not the same. Manifestos, like creeds, are public declarations, but (in accordance with the Latin

Figure 4.1 W. E. B. Du Bois and Shirley Graham Du Bois on his 87th birthday, February 23, 1955. Portrait by photographer Lotte Jacobi in New York. W. E. B. Du Bois Center, the University of Massachusetts, Amherst, W. E. B. Du Bois Papers (MS 312). Used by permission.

root *manifestare*, "to make visible, to disclose") they generally articulate points of policy with regard to a particular cause or causes. Unlike creeds, they are typically lengthy book or pamphlet documents, and for this reason unsuited for communal recitation or repetition. Du Bois's socialist sympathies, especially beginning with his Berlin years (1892–94), were richly nourished by the Marx–Engels *Communist Manifesto* and given eloquent voice in the *Credo*.[3]

Such was the inheritance – the documentary corpus of antecedents and possible models that Du Bois would have known, and with which his and Bonds's respective *Credo*s were in historical and contemporary dialogue. But neither Du Bois nor Bonds would have failed to notice that this inheritance addressed itself principally to the White condition; that it, for all its rich tradition and cultural prestige, essentially ignored the issues, situations, and themes that were distinctive if not unique to Black folk and peoples of color more generally. Their own creeds, the one verbal and the other musical, may thus be regarded as discursive corrections to this racial and social incognizance – an incognizance that, in focusing on White perspective, fails to acknowledge the epistemic apartheid of that perspective in practice and implicitly dismisses the fundamental equality of Black and White by denying that the story of White heritage cannot and must not be told without coequal voicings of the Black condition. Du Bois and Bonds, both individuals committed to (in Bonds's words) "go[ing] farther"[4] than their predecessors in order to better the world for their successors, each undertook to pen a *Credo* that would reconcile these traditionally segregated realms of experience and belief for those who came after them, bequeathing to those successors a verbal and musical inheritance that would manifest their vision for applying their understanding of their Black heritage, with its unique themes and sufferings, in the service of the causes of racial justice and global equality.

Creedal Discourse from Du Bois to Bonds

Du Bois's 1904 *Credo* was the first of a series of significant creeds, manifestos, and platforms that were created and published between then and the release of *Darkwater* in 1920 – all in the service of African American and Black identity and justice generally. The most important of these were the creedal documents of the Niagara Movement (1905) and Oswald Garrison Villard's *The Call* (1909). Each of these creedal documents, like the 1904 *Credo* itself, expressed the overarching idea of social justice for African diasporic people in reasonably compact form and attached that idea to a cause expressed in connection with religion – i.e., with a mandate that emanated from God as a directive to humanity to right a pressing social ailment in order to better the world as a whole.

The first of these movements, the Niagara Movement, was a direct response to the ideological conflict between Du Bois and Booker T. Washington outlined in Chapter 3. It was organized chiefly by Du Bois and the editor of the activist weekly *The Boston Guardian*, Monroe Trotter (1872–1934), with a "Call" written and circulated by Du Bois in June 1905 and an initial private meeting of twenty-nine men in Erie Beach, Ontario, in July of that year. The summons to this meeting called for "organized determination and aggressive action on the part of men who believe in Negro freedom and growth," as well as opposition to "present methods of strangling honest criticism" – a direct swipe at the popularity of Washington's accommodationist approach.[5] The organizers of the movement drafted a "Declaration of Principles" that (not surprisingly, given Du Bois's leadership in the group) echoes themes from the 1904 *Credo* and calls for sweeping reform in the areas of suffrage, civil rights, economic opportunity, the legal system, public opinion, health, employment, war, religion, freedom to assemble and organize, and more. Among its exhortations that assert the sacrality of the cause by association with God:

We repudiate the monstrous doctrine that the oppressor should be the sole authority as to the rights of the oppressed. The Negro race in America[,] stolen, ravished and degraded, struggling up through difficulties and oppression, needs sympathy and receives criticism; needs help and is given hindrance, needs protection and is given mob-violence, needs justice and is given charity, needs leadership and is given cowardice and apology, needs bread and is given a stone. This nation will never stand justified before God until these things are changed.[6]

The Niagara Movement would eventually establish thirty branches in thirty-four of the forty-six states at the time, but Du Bois's insistence that it include women as well as men led to a rift with Trotter, and because of organizational and financial difficulties the Movement began to decline by 1908. It folded entirely in 1910. Nevertheless, it gained national attention and scored several court successes, and these, together with outrage and horror at the race riot in Springfield, Illinois, in August 1908,[7] facilitated the founding of the National Association for the Advancement of Colored People (NAACP) in 1909. The first organizational meeting of that group came about as the result of a document titled "The Call," written by Oswald Garrison Villard (1872–1949), White editor of the *New York Evening Post* and grandson of the great abolitionist William Lloyd Garrison. That appeal, while couched in language that decried how far the legal standing of African Americans had declined since the time of Abraham Lincoln's Emancipation Proclamation (1863), again echoes with remarkable specificity the themes set forth in the nine articles of the *Credo*, so much so that it might be considered a trope on Du Bois's 1904 creed.[8] The response was immediate and widespread, and Du Bois's work as founding member of the NAACP was augmented by his responsibilities as editor of the Association's official journal, *The Crisis*.

The NAACP scored significant legal victories and *The Crisis* flourished under Du Bois's editorship during the decade in which Bonds was born. As a whole, however, the organization's first decade of her life was characterized by extraordinary and dangerous polarization that threatened to tear the world apart in ways that would have been hard to imagine only a few years earlier. The outbreak of World War I unleashed unprecedented violence; and although the United States did not officially enter that war until the spring of 1917, the foreign conflict lent new momentum to the ongoing mass exodus of Black folk from the American South[9] by creating significant factory jobs in the industrialized urban North. Southern Blacks' incentive to move, to leave behind the only land, friends, and family they had ever known, was increased by the dramatic increase of anti-Black violence that attended the resurgence of the Ku Klux Klan, fueled in part by the release of D. W. Griffith's 1915 film *The Birth of a Nation*, which portrayed the Ku Klux Klan as saviors of a valiant post-Civil War South beset by lascivious freed Blacks and northern carpetbaggers.[10] African Americans suffering under the Black codes and the sharecropping and peonage systems of the South found in northward migration new hope as well as incentive for a life that was at least remotely consistent with the freedom and opportunity that Whites enjoyed – but this was possible only through extraordinary hardship and privation, and the South controlled all the legal, financial, and other resources it needed to make departure difficult.[11] These circumstances – specifically the nationally publicized lynchings of Jessie Washington and Ell Persons in Waco, Texas, and Memphis, Tennessee, in 1916 and 1917 as well as the East St. Louis Race Riots of May and July 1917 – combined with the growing sense of solidary among US Blacks to occasion one of the most symbolically potent events of the decade: the Silent Parade of about 10,000 African American men, women, and children on July 28, 1917. And the international attention garnered by that event under Du Bois's leadership further occasioned the first four Pan-African Congresses (Paris, 1919; London, 1921; London, 1923; and New York City, 1927). Indicative of the affirmative side of this dramatically bifurcated situation for US Blacks were two events that directly affected

Bonds: a renewed proliferation of schools, colleges, and academies of music and the arts specifically for Blacks; and the formation of the National Association of Negro Musicians in 1919.[12]

On the whole, the first few years of Margaret Bonds's life tragically proved the wisdom that the anti-racist, anti-colonialist, pacifist Du Bois had set forth in his 1904 *Credo* and elsewhere. For many Southern Blacks, northward migration was born less of the opportunity of the North than the violence of the South; their memory of the violence, racism, and oppression they endured in the South would forever haunt them, even after the events themselves were years behind, even when the soil on which it occurred was hundreds of miles away. Moreover, while migrant Blacks found new opportunity in the urban North, they were still relentlessly exploited by White society, with low wages, crowded and segregated housing, inferior education, and voting power that was limited by gerrymandering. Finally, more than 350,000 African Americans enlisted when the United States entered the war in 1917, but they were assigned to some of the most vulnerable positions in that vicious conflict, and many more were allowed to serve only in menial kitchen and janitorial capacities.[13] This newly invented systemic White exploitation of Black folk (or new iteration of a previously invented system) certainly vindicated the then-controversial position Du Bois had argued in 1915 in an *Atlantic Monthly* essay titled "The African Roots of the War": that the global conflict of World War I was the inevitable result of the apportionment of Africa by the United States and White European powers at the Berlin Conference in 1884; that labor, racism, imperialist exploitation of natural resources, and exploitation of women were the driving motivators for domestic and foreign policy alike in the United States and Europe; and that only by combating those pernicious forces – hardly an objective of the war – could peace be attained.[14] More importantly, the global cataclysm of the war translated Article V of the *Credo* into harsh and often deadly terms, reaffirming for all but the most committed racists that another victory in war would only repeat the timeless historical tragedy of systemic White exploitation of Black labor for White profit:[15]

I believe in the Prince of Peace. I believe that War is Murder. I believe that armies and navies are at bottom the tinsel and braggadocio of oppression and wrong, and I believe that the wicked conquest of weaker and darker nations by nations whiter and stronger but foreshadows the death of that strength.

It was thus not only appropriate, but necessary, for Du Bois to reprint his creed in updated form at the head of his 1920 autobiography, *Darkwater: Voices from within the Veil*. His words now struck the chord of their time: At turns autobiographical, fictional, historical, and sociological, *Darkwater* is an eloquent call to arms for the struggle for civil rights and equality within the United States, a fierce and brilliant denunciation of colonialist exploitation and imperialism, and a summons for all people who fall on the non-White side of the world color line to unite under the banner of the common cause of global equality. Like the *Credo* itself, *Darkwater* is not entirely new, but rather a collage of new material and revised versions of previously published material,[16] brought together now in an experimental form that surely appealed also to the brilliant spirit of innovation that characterized the vibrant cultural and intellectual air created by urbanized Black folk in their newly adopted cities. But newly prominent in it – and surely a reason for its appeal to Margaret Bonds – is its denunciation of the White male world's systemic exploitation of women, especially Black women.

From Inheritance to Heritage: Bonds's Engagement with the Du Bois *Credo*

Among the eventual readers of *Darkwater* was Margaret Bonds. Precisely when she came to know the *Credo* cannot be ascertained, but (as shown in the Introduction) her social sensibilities were cultivated by her mother and finely honed by her awareness of current events. Her correspondence shows that she set to work composing the *Credo* almost immediately after completing *The Montgomery Variations*. By this point she would have been keenly appreciative of the propheticism of Du Bois's text, having spent her entire career working against the effects of racism and economic privation, seen not one or even two, but three major wars (World War II, Korea, and Vietnam) that brought the world color line into conflict, and toured the segregated South during the Civil Rights Movement's critical years of 1963 and 1964. A more compelling view of the depth and significance of Du Bois's understanding and vision is difficult to imagine.

At any rate, Margaret Bonds's correspondence indicates that the piano–vocal version of the *Credo* was complete by August of 1965, i.e., less than a year after she had played *The Montgomery Variations* at the piano for Raoul Abdul. In 1960 or 1961 she had given a manuscript copy of *The Ballad of the Brown King* to Albert McNeil.[17] McNeil gave that work its West coast premiere on December 24, 1961, and he and Bonds remained in close contact to the end of her life.[18] On August 8, 1965 she wrote to Hughes:

Dearest Langston,

The conductor of whom I spoke to you highly approves my latest choral work. It is "Dark Water" [*sic*] and "Credo" of W.E.B. DUBOIS [*sic*]. I sttill [*sic*] have to remain silent. There is the A and R [Artists & Repertoire] man to sell. Now I am in the midst of copying the work … choral parts and piano … and provided we please the A and R man I'll have a side of an RCA Red Seal to be recorded in December. I don't need to tell you what this means to me, and to any project with which I am connected.[19]

Those plans for a recording did not come to fruition – and on October 20, 1965, Bonds wrote to Hughes that this was a blessing, given the US government's increasingly intense efforts to repudiate Du Bois's authority because of his sympathies with Communist ideas:

I'm happy we [i.e., Albert McNeil and I] didn't do Dubois' [*sic*] "Credo." Every day on the radio I hear news of the W.E.B. Du Bois Clubs, and I hear rumor that the government will crush them.[20] I'm not despondent, or hurt, or disappointed. I live so under the guidance of the Divine, I know there had to be reason for me to set those words, so in time, something *good* will happen with "Credo" and sometime in my own mind I "hear it." Ralph [Satz] tells me its [*sic*] a powerful piece – so in God's own time.[21]

The piano–vocal version of Bonds's setting would finally be performed with the composer at the piano by Bonds's friend Frederick Wilkerson (1913–80) in Washington, DC, on March 12, 1967, and indeed, the typed cover of the bound photocopy of this version that Bonds's daughter, Djane Richardson, had in her possession at her death includes at the bottom the note "Frederick Wilkerson Vocal

Studio / 1334 Thirteenth Street, N. W. / Washington, D.C.," suggesting that the studio paid for bound photocopies to be used by the choristers.[22] Bonds reported on this upcoming performance, which apparently was originally scheduled for February 11, 1967, in an important letter to Langston Hughes dated 23 November 1966:

> And then, I guess you know about Frederick Wilkerson's program on February 11, in Washington.
>
> It will represent a cross-section of some of my best produce. I would say that "Three Dream Portraits" are yet undiscovered. *I* know that they represent the kind of creation that may never "buy the creators a herring" – in themselves. But then since a career is a matter of accumulation, they have an extremely important function.
>
> Everything on the program is important – a new piece with poetry by Etienne Grelet [*sic*], Chaney, Frost, Millay[23] – spirituals. I think, however, the W. E. B. Dubois [*sic*] "Credo" will be the star. It's a very serious piece in the American idiom. It has some lines that are controversial – but I'm sure every line contained its Universal Truth – and with my Universal Language – Music – the Public will hear.[24]

In the meantime, Bonds also began work on a version for orchestra on January 12, 1966. This version, intended for use in a planned performance in New York that would have paired the work with *The Ballad of the Brown King* and "other items – choir and orch[estra],"[25] included a brief added introduction that Bonds liked well enough to write out twice – once as a full-score draft in pencil, then in full score that continued into the orchestral version (this autograph also in pencil).[26]

Bonds ultimately abandoned this introduction and the planned performance of the orchestral–choral version alongside *The Ballad of the Brown King* came to naught – but McNeil did perform the orchestral version of the *Credo*, along with *The Montgomery Variations*, with his chorus in San Francisco in 1967. A typescript submitted for the Northwestern University alumni news and dated December 18, 1967, reads:

> MARGARET BONDS. B.M. 1933 AND AM 1934 received signal honors on the West Coast. The McNeil Singers rendered her "Sit Down Servant," at the Statler Hilton in Los Angeles during the NANM Convention. The world premiere of CREDO AND MONTGOMERY VARIATIONS for voices and Orchestra was also performed by the McNeil Singers in San Francisco. Musician friends in Carmel and Van Nuys gave a reception for Margaret Bonds and her teen-age

daughter Djane Richardson during her stay in California for her prowess[,] deeming her Composer of the Year.[27]

At some point Bonds also wrote to Du Bois's widow, Shirley Graham Du Bois (1896–1977), to request permission to use Du Bois's words. This request was granted, although Du Bois's widow reportedly expressed some concern that the text would be ill-received in the United States because of its anti-imperialist, anti-colonialist, anti-racist stance.[28] The 1967 San Francisco performance thus remained the only performance of the orchestral version of the *Credo* during Bonds's lifetime.

That fact is surprising, given the high profile that both Bonds and McNeil enjoyed by 1967, as well as the obvious timeliness of the works. But that very timeliness, and contemporary trends in US attitudes toward Du Bois, may have been the problem (as Shirley Graham Du Bois feared). Certainly the *Credo*'s beautiful affirmations of the dignity of the African American condition and forceful denunciations of bigotry, segregation, and oppression would have resonated powerfully with the Civil Rights Movement; indeed, passages such as No. 6, with its affirmations of the right to vote and the right to education, would have sounded as celebrations of the passage of the landmark Civil Rights Acts of 1964 and 1965, legislative victories that were still recent enough to be savored with joy. Yet these triumphs were also tainted by increasing tragedy – the assassination of Malcolm X and the Watts riots in 1965, widespread and unchecked police brutality against Blacks throughout the United States, rioting in Black communities against these acts of White rage throughout what has come to be known as the "long, hot summer" of 1967, and the assassinations of Robert F. Kennedy and Martin Luther King, Jr., as well as widespread political unrest and violence, throughout 1968.

Additionally, the *Credo*'s outspoken condemnation, in Articles IV and V, of colonialist exploitation and warfare waged by White powers against the non-White side of the world color line would have angered those who supported the ever-more-deadly war of capitalist and colonialist exploitation in Vietnam – the undeclared "American War" (as it is known in Vietnam) that would claim not only 58,220 US lives by the time it ended in 1975, but also, in a stark statistic that confirms Du Bois's and Bonds's condemnation, anywhere between 1 million and 3.1 million Vietnamese lives during that same time period.[29] All of this was, of course, in addition to another casualty of the war: the project of the Great Society itself – as Martin Luther King, Jr. pointed out in a speech he gave on February 25, 1967, just under fourteen months before his own assassination.[30]

This situation was a dilemma for Margaret Bonds and her *Credo*. On the one hand, her renown was reaching new heights. Indeed, it was so great that on January 29, 1967, Northwestern University, home to profoundly hurtful racism during Bonds's years of study there in the early 1930s, awarded her a prestigious Alumni Merit Award, along with other notables including US Senator George McGovern (1972 Democratic nominee for the US presidency). Her return to Chicago was real news – such that Chicago mayor Richard J. Daley marked the occasion by proclaiming January 31, 1967, as the city's official Margaret Bonds Day.[31] On the other hand, while Bonds had never shied away from challenges or controversial causes, neither would it have escaped her that many members of the conservative White society that dominated the world of orchestral performance in the late 1960s would have been avowedly unsympathetic to her *Credo*'s message.

The successes of 1967 were also tainted by a profound loss: the death of Langston Hughes on May 22 of that year. Hughes had been Bonds's closest artistic collaborator and friend for thirty-one years – a personal and artistic confidant whom she described as "like [a] brother," and the person whose *The Negro Speaks of Rivers* she said had "helped save [her]" during her difficult years as a segregated student.[32] The two had worked on numerous important projects small and large, including the *Three Dream Portraits*, the recently published gospel song *When the Dove Enters In*,[33] *Shakespeare in Harlem*, *The Ballad of the Brown King*, and *Simon Bore the Cross*. She had abandoned her orchestration of the *Credo* sixteen months before his death. But now – tellingly, given the consilience between the *Credo* and the themes that characterized her collaborations with Hughes and their correspondence – she finally undertook to write out the orchestrated

Interpreting the *Credo* in Context

work. And on its first page she wrote a dedication to the memory of Hughes and her early friend and mentor, Abbie Mitchell (see Figure 3.1, p. 81).

Langston Hughes may have been part of Bonds's decision to move to New York in 1939, and after his death she was, in the words of Helen Walker-Hill, "ready to be persuaded to leave New York."[34] With her daughter fully grown, she decided to join the migration of thousands of other Black folk to the atmosphere of vibrant culture and progressive politics of Southern California, where she had written her "Destiny" letter twenty-five years earlier, for what was supposed to be another temporary stay.[35] The move turned out to be permanent, however, and now Margaret Bonds began anew much as she had launched her career in New York in 1939. She plunged herself into California's vibrant cultural scene and, her renown already well established, quickly became a prominent figure on the musical scene, composing, concertizing, giving public lectures, pursuing film projects, and – in a return to the educational projects for Black youth that had pervaded her career since the Allied Arts Academy in the 1930s – teaching and serving as musical director for the Los Angeles Inner City Institute. On January 23, 1971, she also reconnected with her piano teacher from her time at Northwestern, Emily Boettcher Bogue, a reunion that produced a generous set of letters between the two, as well as informative diary entries by her former teacher.[36]

Bonds did not forget her inheritance after her return to Los Angeles; quite the contrary. She arranged her earlier setting of Hughes's *I, Too, Sing America* for male chorus, wrote a number of spiritual settings, and began work on an expansive musical (eventually titled *Bitter Laurel*) on the subject of Elizabeth Keckley (1818–1907), the formerly enslaved woman who rose to become dressmaker and confidante of Mary Todd Lincoln as well as an author and activist in the late nineteenth century.[37] In 1969 legendary soprano Leontyne Price, a longtime friend for whom she had already written several spiritual settings, invited her to set four more for her upcoming recital tour and recording with the Rust College Choir, and this invitation resulted in three surviving spiritual settings of great power, beauty, and imagination.[38] In 1971 she completed another large-scale composition: *Scripture*

132

Reading, a set of arrangements of spirituals for narrator and orchestra based on the Old Testament prophets who, as we have seen, were important sources of inspiration for African Americans in their struggle for freedom.[39] Clearly, the astounding energy and creativity of the late California period reveals that Margaret Bonds was beginning a new professional chapter that would have carried further the expansive musical social-justice project that had led to *The Montgomery Variations* and *Credo* – as indeed it had been the driving force of her entire career.

Flex: The Music-Publishing Industry and the Posthumous Obscurity of the *Credo*

Margaret Bonds's setting of the Du Bois *Credo* was the subject of an important dissertation in 2003 and an edition was included in that document,[40] but the work remained unpublished until 2020, when a new, source-critical edition (score and parts) was published on a rental basis by Hildegard Publishing Company in conjunction with Theodore Presser Company.[41] The complete piano–vocal version received its first documented performance in modern memory in February 2022 in an all-Bonds concert given by Grammy-winning chorus Conspirare with soprano Nicole Joseph, bass-baritone Marques Jerrell Ruff, and pianist Anton Nel under the direction of Craig Hella Johnson, and the orchestral version received its modern premiere at Georgetown University in April 2022, with that University's Concert Choir and Orchestra conducted by Angel Gil-Ordoñez. Since then, the piano–vocal version has been performed many times and the orchestral version several times. Like *The Montgomery Variations*, it would seem, the *Credo* has at last found its footing in the same musical world that heard next to nothing of it for the previous half-century. And with both versions now recorded,[42] published in easily available source-critical editions,[43] and circulating in academic as well as professional musical circles, it seems destined to stay.

But the sudden reemergence of Margaret Bonds's *Credo* and the musical world's enthusiasm for it raise one other pressing question: given the renown Margaret Bonds had achieved by the mid-1960s, why was the *Credo* not published during her lifetime?

The composer's surviving correspondence answers that question plainly. It tells a tale of the powerful White-dominated music-publishing industry taking advantage of classical musicians' dependency on printed and published music to ensure that Margaret Bonds's musical racial-justice manifesto would be consigned to archives rather than allowed to proclaim its dangerous message in public. Here is that tale in three letters:

(1) By 1965, Margaret Bonds's and Langston Hughes's cantata *The Ballad of the Brown King*, published by Sam Fox Music in 1961, had become a resounding commercial success, with dozens of performances around the United States and as far as away as Nigeria. Because of its popularity, Margaret Bonds was in a good position to leverage its sales to facilitate another publication with Sam Fox Music. She approached them on September 9, 1965, about publishing the *Credo* and played it at the piano for them on that occasion. The publisher told her that they could not publish the work unless she changed its text – especially that of the second movement ("Especially do I believe in the Negro Race, the beauty of its spirit, the sweetness of its soul, and its strength in that meekness which shall yet inherit this turbulent earth") – and they asked her to request Shirley Graham Du Bois's permission to make those changes to her late husband's text. With obvious discomfort, Bonds reported on that meeting to the poet's widow on September 13, 1965:

Dear Shirley Graham DuBois [*sic*],

It was my happy task to play my setting of Mr. DuBois' [*sic*] "CREDO" for Mr. Fred Fox of Sam Fox Publishing Co., and his Editor, Mr. Ralph Satz on Thursday, Sept. 9. Both gentlemen were deeply impressed and joyful that another cantata of mine is soon to be ready for the market. Mr. Satz knew Mr. DuBois [*sic*] personally and is his devotee.

However, Mr. Fox asks your permission to change some of the words. He assured us that as the text now stands only non-white choirs would use it. These changes would not be drastic; for instance, in place of "Especially do I believe in the Negro race", "Especially do I believe in the Human race" might be used.

I, myself, hate making these changes, but what can one do? This company is the third largest in the field of Educational music, and we don't want anyone to be deprived of singing the cantata who wishes to sing it.

Perhaps we might compromise on having Mr. DuBois [*sic*] original printed on a leaf of the book. . . . or footnotes might be used. Have you any suggestions? . . .

I hope you will clarify in your next letter what you would like us to do concerning the text so that we may move forward in this publication which is so timely. . . . I look forward to the time when "CREDO" will move all over the world.[44]

(2) In a 1990 interview with Helen Walker-Hill, the composer's daughter, Djane Richardson, emphasized that Bonds was "hurt" that Shirley Graham Du Bois believed that she actually *wanted* to change the poet's text;[45] finding herself in an awkward position – change the text and publish the *Credo* or not change it and deny it publication and the resulting performances – she was merely conveying the ultimatum the publisher had given her. In any event, Shirley Graham Du Bois defended her late husband's manifesto emphatically and with legal notice:

My dear Margaret Bonds:

I have your letter of September 13th.

I congratulate you on having finished your music and that it is well received. I regret, however, that my answer to your request must be a categorical "NO."

It is unthinkable that any of the words in Dr. Du Bois' CREDO be changed for presentation. The one example you gave as not being "drastic" cuts the heart out of the CREDO. *"Especially do I believe in the Negro race"* is what my husband was saying all his life. He *returned* to Africa to underline that fact.

Here I would not compromise at any point.

Indeed, I feel so strongly about this that I am sending a copy of this letter to my lawyer in New York with instructions that he write you and Mr. Fox.

I gladly gave you permission to set the CREDO TO music, but not to rewrite it.[46]

Bonds evidently sensed that Sam Fox Music (in the persons of Fred Fox and Ralph Satz) would not bend in their refusal to publish the *Credo* unless its text were changed to words less discomfiting to White folk. Because *The Ballad of the Brown King* was her best-selling published work and the music-publishing industry was otherwise populated almost exclusively by White-owned and -operated firms with whom she had less financial clout than with Sam Fox, there was no reason to expect those firms to be any more willing to publish the *Credo* than Sam Fox was. She therefore set the work's publication aside for the time being and focused on promoting it in performance – a decision that led to the 1967 performances in Washington, DC, and San Francisco (see p. 128–30).

(3) On September 21, 1971, with sales and performances of *The Ballad of the Brown King* still soaring, the solo-piano version of *Troubled Water* selling well, and her other works with other publishers selling well, Bonds reapproached Sam Fox about publishing her setting of the Du Bois *Credo*. That letter does not survive, but Sam

Fox Music's reply, dated November 4, 1971, does – and in it the publisher again damningly refuses to publish Bonds's choral masterpiece unless she changes "Especially do I believe in the Negro Race":

Dear Margaret:

Forgive the delay in answering your letter of September 21st but I did want to discuss the matter you raised with Frederick [Fox] before attempting a reply.

It turned out that he remembered the whole business of your presentation of CREDO a while back and he said that he still feels the same way about the publication of I BELIEVE IN THE NEGRO RACE. Unfortunately, this attitude will prejudice the cause of publication of the entire work. . . .

I'm also a bit disappointed but I could still feel better if you were to turn your enormous knowledge of traditional gospel to use and put out a few choral arrangements for me to publish. I think that the evangelical spirit that exists in the Baptist and AME Churches will prove to be an invigorating experience for any performers, be they black or white.[47]

The exchanges chronicled in these letters are a clear instance of the White music-publishing industry flexing its financial muscle to ensure that words affirming what Du Bois and Bonds termed "the Negro Race" went unheard – unless Bonds "cut the heart out of [the *Credo*]" (as Shirley Graham Du Bois had put it). But by 1971 Bonds's genius for setting spirituals, and the market viability of those settings, was a matter of record, so Sam Fox invited her to send them some spirituals instead of the *Credo* – works that would make them a handsome profit.

Happily, Bonds snubbed that invitation. Instead, she offered the eight spirituals that she had written for Leontyne Price in 1968–70 to Sam Fox Music's biggest rival, Theodore Presser Company.[48] But the damage was done: in closing its doors to Margaret Bonds's *Credo*, Sam Fox Music had again ensured that its (for them) discomfiting musical affirmation of Black folk and the sacrality of the quest for racial justice and global equality would remain in manuscript, unable to be performed for, and heard by, more than a few people at a time, unable to be studied, unable to be taught.

The postlude to that story is one of courage and heartbreak. After Sam Fox's refusal, Margaret Bonds again turned her attention to promoting the *Credo* in performance. Already in August 1971, about three weeks before reapproaching Sam Fox Music about the work, pianist Reginald Fischer, whom she had met in 1965 through her former teacher from Chicago's Coleridge-Taylor Music School,

Tom Theodore Taylor, had promised to introduce Bonds to his friend Zubin Mehta, conductor of the Los Angeles Philharmonic.[49] Fox's renewed refusal to publish the *Credo* with Du Bois's text intact obviously disappointed her – but now she used her connection to Mehta to work for the *Credo*'s promotion in performance, just as she had done after Fox's 1965 refusal. By March 13, McNeil was already rehearsing the *Credo* for performance with the orchestra.[50] Then, on April 23, 1972, Bonds reported: "Today my crippled friend, Reginald Fisher[,] is having a party where I'm to meet the heads of the Los Angeles Symphony [*sic*]. I'm told Mehta is soon performing my 'Credo.' We shall see!"[51]

But she never did "see." Three days later, on April 26, 1972, Margaret Bonds died of a heart attack, alone in her apartment. She was found by friends two days later – on her knees,[52] as if in prayer.

***

Margaret Bonds heard the orchestral version of her *Credo* only once, at McNeil's San Francisco performance in 1967; the work was still unpublished when she died. Mehta and the Los Angeles Philharmonic planned a full performance as part of a musical tribute to Malcolm X on May 21, 1972, just weeks after the composer's death, but fears that this program would be too controversial led to the concert's being re-themed as "A Tribute to Black Music" and the *Credo* being performed only in excerpt (Nos. 1, 2, 6, and 7).[53] Finally, then, McNeil arranged for a performance of the work in its entirety, given by the Compton Civic Symphony Orchestra and his chorus, the Los Angeles Jubilee Singers, under the direction of Hans Lampl (1919–2013) on April 29, 1973.

That performance was attended by Shirley Graham Du Bois herself, whose staunch defense of her late husband's creed had derailed Sam Fox's attempt to corrupt it in 1965. Now the poet's widow vindicated Margaret Bonds's own bravery in setting, with unflinching honesty, a text whose obvious fearlessness in challenging the systemic racism and "devilish" colonialist exploitation of Black folk everywhere she knew would prove controversial in the White-dominated classical-music establishment. Labeling McNeil's 1973 performance "one of the most moving moments of [her] life,"

Shirley Graham Du Bois described Margaret Bonds's *Credo* as "a work of art that is eternal – that will live as long as people love each other and really believe in brotherhood."[54]

Notes

1. Du Bois was raised in one of the Congregational churches of Great Barrington, Massachussetts, and drew heavily on this upbringing throughout his career. His statement, toward the end of his life, that "the greatest gift of the Russian Federation to the modern world" was its refusal to "allow any church of any kind to interfere with education" and to forbid of the teaching of religion in state schools has been construed as anti-Christian, but in fact it is a critique only of Christianity that does allow that interference and insists that religion be taught in school. While he was agnostic in his final years, this was the final station in a religious identity that evolved continually over the course of his long life, and in fact, religious themes – handled with characteristic originality – permeate his writings of every sort. Writings such as "Jesus Christ in Texas" W. E. B. Du Bois, *Darkwater: Voices from within the Veil* [New York: Harcourt, Brace, and Howe, 1920], 123–33) make clear his scorching contempt for institutions and individuals who professed Christianity even as they practiced hateful and oppressive tactics antithetical to the teachings of Christ, certainly; but rejection of institutions and individuals is not the same as rejection of the faith they misrepresent. See Herbert Aptheker, "W. E. B. Du Bois and Religion: A Brief Reassessment," *Journal of Religious Thought* 39, no. 1 (1982): 5–11; further, Reiland Rabaka, "Du Bois and the Sociology of Religion: The Sociology of the Souls of Religious Black (among Other) Folk," in his *Against Epistemic Apartheid: W. E. B. Du Bois and the Disciplinary Decadence of Sociology* (London: Rowman & Littlefield, 2010), 223–63; and Phil Zuckerman (ed.), *Du Bois on Religion* (Walnut Creek, CA: Rowman & Littlefield, 2000).
2. Margaret Bonds, "Lecture for THE QUEST CLUB," Booth Family Center for Special Collections, Margaret Bonds Papers, GTM-130530, Box 18, folder 4, p. 2. Although Bonds's academic records are protected by privacy law, the University Bulletins of her time at Northwestern suggest that her musical education was quite traditional and more geared toward music theory than toward history. As an undergraduate she was required to take a one-semester overview of music history taught by Oliver Seth Beltz (1887–1978), a Northwestern University alumnus who was an influential figure in the Seventh-Day Adventist Church and would complete his master's degree at Northwestern in 1935 with a thesis on sixteenth-century hymnody

and his PhD in Musicology at the same university in 1944 (this with a dissertation titled "German Religious Radicalism from 1522 to 1535"). This was followed by a two-semester survey of music history, these taught by George Edward McClay, a Northwestern University alumnus who had received his BMusEd. degree in 1928 and would receive his MM there in 1939. These music-history courses were complemented by one course on sight singing and notation, two courses in ear training, two courses in harmony, and further courses in harmonic analysis, (musical) aesthetics, form, counterpoint, and orchestration. As a master's student she was required to take, in addition to further courses in music theory, form, and composition, two semesters of music history taught by McClay. See *Northwestern University Bulletin: University Register, 1929–1930* [Chicago]: Northwestern University, [1929], 489, 495; *Northwestern University Bulletin: University Register for the College Year 1933–1934* [Chicago]: Northwestern University, [1933]. Her junior recital and master's recital are generally of an academic bent, including canonical Western European male composers, but her senior recital is unusual in that it includes no music written before 1890 and is overwhelmingly dedicated to modernist compositions, including the Hornpipe from *The Triumph of Neptune* (1926) by Lord Berners; one of the *Saudades de Brasil* (1927) of Villa-Lobos; the Tango from Erwin Schulhoff's (1894–1942) *Esquisses de jazz* (1928); and the two-piano version of John Alden Carpenter's Concertino for Piano and Orchestra (1920). After leaving Northwestern, the main two canonical compositions she retained in her repertoire were Robert Schumann's *Papillons* (which she had performed in 1931) and César Franck's *Prelude, Chorale, and Fugue,* compositions that were counterbalanced by modernist works, Bonds's own arrangements of spirituals, and music by Black composers. These recital programs are held in the Margaret Bonds file in the Northwestern University Archives (Evanston, Illinois).

3. On Du Bois's early exposure to Marx's work, see Herbert Aptheker, *W.E.B. Du Bois: A Life in American History* (Santa Barbara, CA: ABC-CLIO, 2019), 16–18.

4. Margaret Bonds to Lawrence Richardson, December 17, 1942 (see Chapter 1, p. 23).

5. See David Levering Lewis, *W. E. B. Du Bois: Biography of a Race, 1868–1919* (New York: Henry Holt, 1993), 316.

6. For the complete text of the *Declaration*, see [W.E.B. Du Bois], "The Niagara Movement's 'Declaration of Principles,' 1904," *Black History Bulletin* 68, no. 1 (2005): 21–23.

7. The Springfield Race Riot took place on August 14–16, 1908: over those three days, some 5,000 White residents of the Illinois capital shot innocent Blacks, burned their homes, looted stores, and lynched and

mutilated two elderly Black residents: at least eight Black men were killed by the mob, and it took 4,000 members of the Illinois State Militia to quell the uprising. See James L. Crouthamel, "The Springfield Race Riot of 1908," *Journal of Negro History* 45 (1960): 164–81.

8. See Mary White Ovington, *How the National Association for the Advancement of Colored People Began* (New York: National Association for the Advancement of Colored People, 1914), 3.

9. According to the US Bureau of Census, during the decade 1900–1909 170,000 Blacks moved from the South to the North, and that figure would more than double to 450,000 during the decade 1910–19. An astonishing 750,000 more would migrate during the 1920s. See Stewart E. Tolnay and E. M. Beck, "Rethinking the Role of Racial Violence in the Great Migration," in *Black Exodus: The Great Migration from the American South*, ed. Alferdteen Harrison (Jackson: University Press of Mississippi, 1991), 20–35 at 20. See also Nicholas Lemann, *The Promised Land: The Great Black Migration and How It Changed America* (New York: A. A. Knopf, 1991); and Isabel Wilkerson, *The Warmth of Other Suns: The Epic Story of America's Great Migration* (New York: Random House, 2010).

10. On the significance of *The Birth of a Nation* and the NAACP's immediate and long-term response to it, see especially chapter 1 ("The Birth of a Cultural Strategy") in Jenny Woodley, *Art for Equality: The NAACP's Cultural Campaign for Civil Rights* (Lexington: University Press of Kentucky, 2014), 11–34.

11. See chapter 2 ("Derailing the Great Migration") in Carol Anderson, *White Rage: The Unspoken Truth of Our Racial Divide* (New York: Bloomsbury, 2016), 39–66.

12. Margaret Bonds's mother, Estella, was a charter faculty member of the Coleridge-Taylor Music School, which opened in Chicago in 1913. See Brian Dolinar (ed.), *The Negro in Illinois: The WPA Papers* (Urbana: University of Illinois Press, 2013), 225; further, Eileen Southern, *The Music of Black Americans: A History*, 3rd ed. (New York: W. W. Norton, 1997), 311–12.

13. See especially Chad L. Williams, "The Hell of War: African American Soldiers in Labor and Combat," in his *Torchbearers of Democracy: African American Soldiers in the World War I Era* (Chapel Hill: University of North Carolina Press, 2010), 105–44; and Tyler Stovall, "The Color Line behind the Lines: Racial Violence in France during the Great War," *American Historical Review* 103 (1998): 737–69.

14. W. E. B. Du Bois, "The African Roots of the War," in David Levering Lewis, *W.E.B. Du Bois: A Reader* (New York: Henry Holt, 1995), 642–51. An updated version of this essay was included

as the third section of *Darkwater*; see Bill V. Mullen, *W.E.B. Du Bois: Revolutionary across the Color Line* (London: Pluto Press, 2016), esp. 46–51.

15. See Shane A. Smith, "*The Crisis* in the Great War: W. E. B. Du Bois and His Perception of African-American Participation in World War I," *Historian* 70 (2008): 239–62.

16. See Eric J. Sundquist's introduction to Darkwater in his *The Oxford W.E.B Du Bois: Reader* (New York: Oxford, 1986), 482.

17. Brenda Jean Mohr, "The Life and Legacy of Albert McNeil and the Albert McNeil Jubilee Singers" (DMA diss., University of Washington, 2017), 216.

18. Bonds reports on McNeil's performance in a letter to Langston Hughes dated November 27, 1961 (Yale JWJ MSS 151, Box 16, folder 376: no. 310), and the performance was advertised in *The California Eagle* (December 21, 1965): 5. On November 30, 1964, Bonds wrote to Hughes that she was "living in semi-seclusion to finish [her] largest symphonic score today" (Bonds [New York] to Hughes [New York], Yale JWJ MSS 26, Box 16, folder 380: no. 480). Helen Walker-Hill (*Spirituals to Symphonies*, 170) surmises that this is a reference to the *Credo*, but it is more likely a reference to Bonds's final work on *The Montgomery Variations* (which Walker-Hill wrongly conjectures to have been written later, in 1965).

19. Georgetown University Libraries, Margaret Bonds papers, shelf-mark GTM-130530 Box 1, folder 58.

20. Because of Du Bois's influence, the US government's concern that his lifelong support for socialist causes and refusal to repudiate communism spiked to a new level when he joined the American Communist Party in 1961. See. Bill V. Mullen, *W.E.B. Du Bois: Revolutionary across the Color Line* (London: Pluto Press, 2016); further, Theodore Kornweibel, Jr., *"Seeing Red": Federal Campaigns against Black Militancy, 1919–1925* (Bloomington: Indiana University Press, 1998), 54–75; and Part IV ("The East Is Red: Revolutions and Resolutions") in Bill V. Mullen and Cathryn Watson (eds.), *W.E.B. Du Bois on Asia* (Jackson: University Press of Mississippi, 2005), 169–201.

21. Bonds (Maywood, Illinois) to Hughes (New York), Yale JWJ 26, Box 17, folder 381: no. 513 (also quoted, with minor errors, in Walker-Hill, *Spirituals to Symphonies*, 170).

22. Georgetown University Libraries, Margaret Bonds papers, shelf-mark GTM-130530 Box 13, folder 1.

23. Étienne de Grellet du Mabillier, also known as Stephen Grellet (1773–1855); Robert Frost (1874–1963); Edna St. Vincent Millay (1892–1950). The Grellet piece is *I Shall Pass through this World but Once* (New York: Bourne, 1967). The Frost piece would be

either *Stopping by Woods on a Snowy Evening* or *The Pasture* (see *Rediscovering Margaret Bonds: Art Songs, Spirituals, Musical Theater and Popular Songs*, ed. Louise Toppin (Ann Arbor: Videmus, 2021); the Millay piece could have been any of the six songs on Millay's texts (see *Margaret Bonds, Six Songs on Poems by Edna St. Vincent Millay*, ed. John Michael Cooper [Worcester, MA: Hildegard Publishing, 2020]). Roger Chaney (1928–81) was a lyricist and frequent collaborator of Bonds, but none of her compositions is a clear candidate for this performance.

24. Bonds (New York) to Hughes (New York), November 23, 1966 (Columbia College, Chicago, Helen Walker-Hill papers, Box 5, Series 4, folder 8.5).

25. Bonds (New York) to Hughes (New York), January 14, 1966 (Columbia College, Chicago, Helen Walker-Hill papers, Box 5, Series 4, folder 8.5): "[William] Warfield's concert was superb, and in the Bar at a party given in his honor I talked about Dubois' [*sic*] 'Credo.' Rev. Lawrence is sold on presenting it. I would like to do an entire Bonds program with 'Credo,' 'The Ballad' – and other items – choir and orch[estra]. So, late at night I score a few bars of 'Credo,' and I'm so happy the orchestral accomp[animent] of 'The Ballad' – is finished and ready to use."

26. Georgetown University Libraries, Margaret Bonds papers, shelfmark GTM-130530 Box 13, folder 1.

27. Northwestern University Libraries, Margaret Bonds file.

28. See Rollo Augustus Dilworth, "The *Credo* of Margaret Bonds: An Historical Commentary, Modern Performing Edition, and Conductor's Study" (DM thesis, Northwestern University, 2003), 10.

29. US casualty statistics are from National Archives and Records Administration, "Vietnam War U.S. Military Fatal Casualty Statistics," www.archives.gov/research/military/vietnam-war/casualty-statistics (accessed March 1, 2021). For the Vietnamese casualties and a discussion of the methodological issues that account for the widely varying figures, see Charles Hirschman, Samuel Preston, and Vu Manh Loi, "Vietnamese Casualties During the American War: A New Estimate," *Population and Development Review* 21 (1995): 783–812 at 807.

30. Martin Luther King, Jr., "The Casualties of the Vietnam War," *Atlantic MLK Special Edition* (2018): 92–96.

31. Correspondence concerning Bonds's nomination for and acceptance of this award is found in the Margaret Bonds file of the Northwestern University Libraries. The award itself was presented by the university's president, J. Roscoe Miller, on January 29, 1967, and this ceremony was followed on January 31 by an all-Bonds concert sponsored by the Chicago Music Association with support from Bonds's own Alpha Kappa Alpha sorority and the Senior Choir of Berean Baptist Church;

Bonds also played some of her own piano compositions in this concert. A detailed story previewing the events was published in the Chicago weekly *New Crusader* on January 28, 1967.

32. Walker-Hill, *Spirituals to Symphonies*, 156.
33. Margaret Bonds, *When the Dove Enters In*, ed. John Michael Cooper (Worcester, MA: Hildegard Publishing, 2021).
34. Walker-Hill, *Spirituals to Symphonies*, 155.
35. This late return to Los Angeles has sometimes been described as a symptom of the failure of Bonds's marriage, but this appears to be an exaggeration. Bonds's 1967 move to California did turn out to be permanent rather than temporary and Larry Richardson never did join her there, but the correspondence between the two betrays no signs of bitterness or rancor, plans were occasionally laid for Richardson to visit Bonds in California, and he regularly sent her packages as well as money to help her meet expenses. Aside from apartness itself, the usual signs of marital troubles that lead to separation are not present.
36. Northwestern University Archive, Emily Boettcher Bogue (1907–92) Papers, 19/3/6. These papers include, in addition to letters and a signed photograph from Bonds to Emily Boettcher Bogue, Bogue's diaries for 1971 and 1972, describing her encounters with Bonds and her receipt of the news of her student's death.
37. Originally titled *Madame 'Lisbeth* and written to lyrics by Janice Lovoos, Edmund Penney, and Demetrios Villan on a book by Villan, *Bitter Laurel* eventually encompassed nineteen musical numbers. The complete libretto survives in the Yale Bonds papers (JWJ 151 Box 12, folder 72). The musical numbers survive in the Beinecke Rare Book and Manuscript Library (Yale University), the Booth Family Center for Special Collections (Georgetown University Libraries), and the Schomburg Center for Research in Black Culture (New York Public Library).
38. The three surviving spiritual arrangements are *Sinner, Please Don't Let This Harvest Pass*, *We Shall Overcome*, and *I Wish I Knew How It Would Feel to Be Free*. Price's letter of November 12, 1969, inviting Bonds to arrange the works survives in Yale JWJ 151, Box 12, folder 75. *We Shall Overcome* was published (ed. John Michael Cooper) in Hildegard Publishing Company's Margaret Bonds Signature Series in January 2023, and the other two spirituals are to be published in 2023–24.
39. The *Scripture Reading* was premiered on October 22, 1971, by the Little Symphony of the San Francisco Symphony Orchestra under the direction of Nicklaus Wyss; see *The Times* (San Mateo, CA), October 18, 1971: 29. The program for this concert survives in the

Georgetown University Bonds Papers, shelfmark GTM-130530, Box 5, folder 7.

40. Dilworth, "The *Credo* of Margaret Bonds" (see n. 28).
41. Margaret Bonds, *Credo*, ed. John Michael Cooper (Worcester, MA: Hildegard Publishing Company, 2020).
42. The piano–vocal version has been recorded by Baker L. Purdon and Tenēo (2022) and Justin Smith and the Portland Phoenix Chamber Choir (2023). The choral–orchestral version has been recorded by Malcolm J. Merriweather and The Dessoff Choirs (2023) and Craig Johnson and Conspirare (2023).
43. Margaret Bonds, *Credo: for Soprano, Baritone Solo, SATB Chorus and Piano; Text by W.E.B Du Bois*, ed. John Michael Cooper, Margaret Bonds Signature Series (Worcester, MA: Hildegard Publishing Company, 2022); Margaret Bonds, *Credo: For Soprano, Baritone Solo, SATB Chorus and Orchestra; Text by W.E.B. Du Bois – Study Score* (Worcester, MA: Hildegard Publishing Company, 2023).
44. Bonds (New York) to Shirley Graham Du Bois (Accra), September 13, 1965 (Manuscripts, Archives and Rare Books Division, Schomburg Center for Research in Black Culture, The New York Public Library, Margaret Bonds Papers shelfmark MG873, Box 3, folder 13).
45. Djane Richardson, recorded interview with Helen Walker-Hill, Helen Walker-Hill Collection, Columbia College, Chicago, Tape 16.
46. Shirley Graham Du Bois (Accra) to Bonds (New York), ca. October 1965 (Manuscripts, Archives and Rare Books Division, Schomburg Center for Research in Black Culture, The New York Public Library, Margaret Bonds Papers shelfmark MG873, Box 3, folder 14).
47. Ralph Satz (New York) to Bonds (New York), November 4, 1971 (Manuscripts, Archives and Rare Books Division, Schomburg Center for Research in Black Culture, The New York Public Library, Margaret Bonds Papers shelfmark MG873, Box 3, folder 23).
48. Margaret Bonds, interview with James Hatch, December 28, 1971, Oral History Interview Recordings of the Camille Billops and James V. Hatch Archives, Emory University (shelfmarks HB279.1 and HB279.2).
49. Letter from Bonds (Los Angeles) to Djane Richardson (New York), August 26, 1971 (Manuscripts, Archives and Rare Books Division, Schomburg Center for Research in Black Culture, The New York Public Library, Margaret Bonds Papers shelfmark MG873, Box 2, folder 10).
50. Letters from Bonds to Djane Richardson, August 26, 1971, and March 13, 1972 (Manuscripts, Archives and Rare Books Division,

Schomburg Center for Research in Black Culture, The New York Public Library, Margaret Bonds Papers shelfmark MG873, Box 2, folder 10).

51. Letter from Bonds to Djane Richardson, April 23, 1972 (Manuscripts, Archives and Rare Books Division, Schomburg Center for Research in Black Culture, The New York Public Library, Margaret Bonds Papers shelfmark MG873, Box 2, folder 10).

52. Albert McNeil interview with Helen Walker-Hill, cited in Jackson, "Margaret Bonds and *The Ballad of the Brown King*," 21.

53. See Dilworth, "The *Credo* of Margaret Bonds," 11–12, 182–85.

54. David Levinson, "An Eternal Work of Art," *The Independent*, Long Beach, California (May 1, 1973).

THE VEIL AND MARGARET BONDS'S
SYNCRETIC DUAL PERSPECTIVE

Margaret Bonds, W. E. B. Du Bois, Langston Hughes, Martin Luther King, Jr., Raoul Abdul, Adele Addison, Betty Allen, Eugene Brice, Harry Burleigh, Will Marion Cook, Shirley Graham Du Bois, Nora Holt, Albert McNeil, Abbie Mitchell, Leontyne Price, Booker T. Washington: diversity of occupation and outlook notwithstanding, the principal characters of this book and most of the supporting ones shared the same side of the world color line – and this, more than their genius and talent, defined their lives and livelihoods, their works and their relationship to the world around them. Indeed, that spuriously monochromatic definition of their identity and its translation into wholesale preconception, prejudice, and hatred also forced them into another, and equally potent, societal construct – that of caste. These two constructs, race and caste, were facts of life as unrelenting as they were malevolent, and these individuals' respective resistances to their malevolence as illustrious as hard-won. The tide of lynchings and race riots fueled by White rage was as real as the sixty-five years' worth of writings Du Bois produced in celebration of the inherent human dignity and beauty of Blackness and the cause of global equality. The segregation that followed Margaret Bonds wherever she went at Northwestern University was as real as the beauty and power of the poetry of Langston Hughes that she discovered in the basement of the Evanston Public Library and the creative friendship that was born of it. The firehoses, police dogs, bombings, and burning crosses that populated the Southern landscapes Bonds toured with the Melodaires were as real as the music of peace, redemption, and indeed hope that that violence inspired her to write. And the chances of Black folk being able to persuade the United States' patently White male dominated culture of classical music to accept major orchestral and choral works by a Black woman were as small as those works themselves were manifestly brilliant.

Taken together, these conditions meant that the main characters in this book, and Black folk generally, were united also by another condition that fueled their creative imaginations even as it enabled them to withstand the forces of the systemic racism that sought to subjugate those creative imaginations, indeed their entire existence. That condition is what Du Bois, in his seminal 1903 *The Souls of Black Folk*, termed a "double-consciousness." In Du Bois's conception, Blacks sense this "two-ness" as viewing themselves through a "veil" that, although imposed by the ways in which they are viewed by the non-Black world, is a gift that endows them with second-sight that would be impossible without it:

After the Egyptian and Indian, the Greek and Roman, the Teuton and Mongolian, the Negro is a sort of seventh son, born with a veil, and gifted with second-sight in this American world, – a world which yields him no true self-consciousness, but only lets him see himself through the revelation of the other world. It is a peculiar sensation, this double-consciousness, this sense of always looking at one's self through the eyes of others, of measuring one's soul by the tape of a world that looks on in amused contempt and pity. One ever feels his two-ness, – an American, a Negro; two souls, two thoughts, two unreconciled strivings; two warring ideals in one dark body, whose dogged strength alone keeps it from being torn asunder.[1]

As *The Souls of Black Folk* and Du Bois's subsequent writings make clear, this double-consciousness created by Blacks in response to the prejudice and ignorance of non-Blacks is a socioeconomic construct, not one that is physiologically or psychologically inherent in the condition of Blackness, and it means that Black folk inevitably view the world, with all its preconceptions and prejudices, surging triumphs and searing defeats, with a "second-sight" that they constantly strive to render unnecessary. For Blacks such as Margaret Bonds, it meant that the "refusals in restaurants, suspicious glances from shopkeepers and other insults to the quote American way of life,"[2] the poetry and music, and the profound segregation that struggled to oppress Black creative imagination and segregate Black music from White were the seed of a different, and necessarily extraordinarily complex, artistic productivity – one that could arise only from within that veil.

Bonds publicly hinted (with characteristic edgy humor) at her own experience of this "two-ness" in two different ways in her public statements. Her 1967 *Reminiscence*, discussed in Chapter 1, offers some insights into her personal experience of it and the issues it posed for her in her relationships with other musicians and the public generally. The central theme of those remarks is the centrality of Blackness to Bonds's musical identity: she articulates this in terms of her early associations with Abbie Mitchell and the music of Harry Burleigh, her immediate and deeply personal identification with Langston Hughes's poetic celebrations of the inherent beauty and humanity of Blackness, her studies with William Levi Dawson and Florence Price, and her indebtedness to the stylistic eclecticism of Will Marion Cook. She also empha-sizes a deeply religious nature as definitive for Black identity – from her mother's identity as "a true woman of God" to the success of the prayers of the "God-loving people" who "would 'jump-to'" in order to help Price and Bonds with their musical projects, to the general assertion that "the 'so-called Negro' in America" in the 1960s was "Judeo-Christian by religion."[3]

Yet interwoven with the theme of Bonds's African American *personal* identity in that *Reminiscence* is the issue of how these Black aspects of her *musical* identity created problems for her in the White-dominated concert-music world – and, indeed, even among African Americans. She initially recounts how an early, unidentified teacher and even Marian Anderson found the "jazzy augmented chords" of the closing section of *The Negro Speaks of Rivers* off-putting, then states that legendary French pedagogue Nadia Boulanger (1887–1979) "refused to take [her] as a student" even though "whatever [she] was doing" "'felt right to her.'" She describes the African American of the late 1960s as "a marginal-ized person" and seems to attribute this marginalization to a conflict between the lived experiences and lived sufferings of African Americans on the one hand and the dominance of European training in education and culture on the other: "[The Black American's] influences, if he is educated, are mostly European. He uses European techniques to express his talents. What other techniques could he possibly know?" And she portrays the connection she draws between Cook's influence and

Boulanger's refusal to take her as a student as emblematic of this compulsory conflict of musical identity: "Even now, when I write something for a choir and it's jazzy and bluesy and spiritual and Tchaikovsky all rolled up into one, I laugh to myself, 'That is Will Marion Cook.' No wonder Boulanger didn't quite understand what my music is all about."[4]

But if the veil as perceived and described with painful and majestic eloquence by Du Bois is, as Reiland Rabaka has noted, a patently social and cognitive product of the condition of alterity forced upon the lived worlds, lived experiences, and lived endurances of out-groups and the Black oppressed,[5] then Margaret Bonds's correspondence and public statements demonstrate that, for her, existence within the spheres of concert music was doubly veiled because she was a woman. This theme emerges in her 1940s correspondence with Larry Richardson, there invited by the societally imposed inequities in marriage and male–female relationships in general, and the defiant tone given voice as she declares her sense of maternal heritage and responsibility articulates this theme. The 1942 "Destiny" letter is also consistent with it: citing the obstacles that her ancestors had "silently, quietly, in obscurity" overcome "for our oppressed Race," she aligns herself above all with her maternal lineage as she declares that she "shall fulfill [her] Destiny" and "go farther."[6] But in the 1960s, as second-wave feminism gained traction, Bonds more frequently and frankly focused on the obstacles the male-dominated world of concert music placed before her because of her sex:

I am a musician and a humanitarian . . . [but] people don't really think a woman can successfully compete in this field [of concert music]. . . . Women are expected to be wives, mothers and do all the nasty things in the community (Oh, I do them), and if a woman is cursed with having talent, too, then she keeps apologizing for it.[7]

This double veil was not unique to Bonds; far from it – and the demographics of orchestral performance life and audience demographics in the 1960s and early 1970s make clear that, for Blacks and women throughout the United States (and beyond), the large-scale symphonic and choral/orchestral scoring represented in *The Montgomery Variations* and *Credo* was a direct challenge to the system of racial and sexual subjugation of which Bonds speaks – to both of the veils that informed her experience of the world of concert music.

Nowhere is the physicality of the first of these veils (the racial one described by Du Bois) more obvious than in the infrastructure of the orchestral world itself. For most of Bonds's career that world was no less segregated – by law and by other practices unwritten but all the more powerful for that reason – than its surrounding society was. In the Jim Crow South, Blacks were excluded from the realms of formal concert music populated and attended by Whites, and even in the urban north the segregational structure of life Othered people of color at every turn, from entry into concert halls to the vanishingly small presence of concert music by Black composers in programs and Black faces on the stages themselves. Few prejudices could be more profoundly and disturbingly racist (and historically false) than the widespread White assumptions that people of color only produce and practice dances and other vernacular musics; that when people of color create and consume concert music that does not use these idioms it is by definition inauthentic, inferior, or some sort of selling-out.[8] But those assumptions are as irrational as the institutionalized hatreds and dehumanizing exploitations of the world color line itself – so Black Americans celebrated Black genius in their own refusal to comply with them. They responded to them affirmatively in separatist solutions, by creating their own institutions for concert as well as vernacular music – most importantly institutions such as the National Association of Negro Musicians (founded in 1919), but also opera companies (the Reconstruction-era Colored American Opera Company founded in 1873, the Drury Grand Opera Company, the Aeolian Opera Association, the National Negro Opera Company, and, in 1971, Opera-South) and orchestras (the Lyre Club Symphony Orchestra, the Clef Club Symphony Orchestra, and the Symphony of the New World).[9] Much of the credit for willing these institutions into existence – through education, journalism, community organizing, and more – belongs to women.[10]

These and other such institutions could have provided a reasonable venue for the performance of *The Montgomery*

Epilogue

Variations and *Credo* – and as shown in Chapter 4, Bonds's close relationship with Albert McNeil produced expectations (never realized) that the *Credo* would be recorded with him and the Los Angeles Jubilee Singers. On the whole, however, NANM-sponsored programs were for soloists and chamber ensembles, not orchestra or orchestra with chorus. Other options for having large orchestral and orchestral–choral works performed by Black ensembles for Black audiences – i.e., performers and listeners who would understand them from within the Du Boisian veil – were few.

In the context of an American orchestral infrastructure and musical life that historically were deeply segregated, this meant that most practical performance venues for *The Montgomery Variations* and *Credo* were predominantly White. Although reliable data for the mid-1960s is scarce, data from earlier points in US history is remarkably consistent with its counterparts from the 1970s, advances in civil rights law made during the 1960s notwithstanding. As a benchmark, the 1960 United States census reported that in that year Blacks constituted 10.52 percent of the population (18,871,831 out of 179,323,175 persons counted), and in 1970 the same report documented Blacks as constituting 11.92 percent of the population (22,539,362 out of 203,210,158).[11] In the absence of concrete data, we must tentatively assume that at the midpoint of that decade (the year after the completion of *The Montgomery Variations* and the beginning of Bonds's work on the *Credo*) Blacks constituted the median of these two percentages – i.e., 11.22 percent.[12] But the percentage of Blacks in White US orchestras did not even approach these benchmarks: a 1974 survey of fifty-four US orchestras with budgets of over USD $1 million found only sixty-seven "minority" musicians among the 4,690 musicians hired on a regular basis – 1.4 percent, just over one-tenth of what it should have been using general population demographics as a benchmark.[13]

A similar dilemma confronted Bonds with the womanist themes in her music – themes that are only subtly present in *The Montgomery Variations* but more obvious in the *Credo*. The late nineteenth and twentieth centuries witnessed the formation of many women's orchestras that were in some ways counterparts to the specifically Black organizations mentioned earlier. By charter and intent, these organizations rebuked the institutionalized sexism of the White male mainstream of orchestral life by assuring women a space in which to make concert music rather than forcing them to submit to sexist male hegemony. Perhaps the best known and (for purposes of this book) most relevant of these orchestras is the Woman's Symphony Orchestra of Chicago – the group with which Bonds performed Florence Price's Piano Concerto in One Movement in 1934;[14] others include the Cleveland Women's Orchestra and the Women's Symphony Association of Lancaster, Pennsylvania. Among mainstream orchestras, many of which are ostensibly gender-integrated, although women constitute approximately 50.5 percent of the population, US orchestras with budgets of over USD $1 million employed an average of just 18.3 percent women in the 1964–65 season, a figure that had risen to 21.8 percent a decade later.[15] Both figures are less than half of what they ought to be. Although the biases were less pronounced in orchestras with smaller budgets (i.e., regional, collegiate, and community orchestras) and the *Credo*, as shown in Chapter 4, eventually was premiered by one such orchestra, the length and difficulty of both compositions does not lend itself to amateur performance.

In other words: when Margaret Bonds wrote *The Montgomery Variations* and *Credo* – two sizable and difficult musical civil rights manifestos with Black feminist themes – she had to assume her performers would be at least 95 percent White and 85 percent male. That was a formidable challenge, for concepts such as *integration* and *feminism* were subjects of heated political and artistic debate. Bonds could by no means assume that most of those presumably White male performers would be sympathetic to the exhortations for racial and gender justice that are the raisons d'être of her compositions. What was she thinking?

Two powerful models for this strategy would have been within her realm of experience – one from within the domain of music, the other from her ancestral heritage. The first is what Jeffrey Sposato, in connection with the music of Felix Mendelssohn Bartholdy, has termed the "strategy of dual perspective," referring to Mendelssohn's own manner of reconciling his Jewish heritage and Lutheran faith for listeners both Christian and Jewish in the increasingly anti-Semitic world of nineteenth-century Europe. Mendelssohn employed both Jewish and Christian texts, musical styles, subjects, and rhetorics simultaneously, thereby enabling his music to be understandable, and sympathetic, to both sides of that theologically and culturally riven world, each from its own perspective.[16] This strategy, as Sposato points out, depended in large part on performers and listeners from either side of that ideological chasm being able to recognize their own perspective in Mendelssohn's art. While Margaret Bonds could not have anticipated a theorizing of Mendelssohn's strategy that was formulated well after her death, her musical education at Northwestern would have acquainted her with his choral music where this strategy of dual perspective was most pronounced, especially *Elijah*. Moreover, she had, as we have seen, a pronounced sense of history, historical legacy, and the importance of religious belief for the composer's work, and she not only worked on behalf of Jewish causes but also lived through the revelation of the horrors that had been committed in Nazi-dominated Europe in the 1930s and 1940s. That Margaret Bonds would have failed to empathize with Mendelssohn's deeply Christian faith, been ignorant of his Jewish heritage, or not seen him as a musical personification of the casualties of cultural, political, musical, and theological prejudice is improbable – and so she may well have recognized and appreciated his strategic reconciliation of seemingly irreconcilable Jewish and Christian themes in his music.[17]

The other possible model for Margaret Bonds's syncretic musical handling of her identity as African American and woman in the exclusionary idioms of male-dominated White concert music came specifically from her Black ancestral history in the United States – specifically, from the rich legacy of Black preachers and orators who bested the racist proselytizing of their White Christian oppressors by mastering not only the Bible but also the rhetorics that the oppressors used to rationalize their oppression. Here, too, the contradiction is – as in *The Montgomery Variations* – one in which faith and morality are profoundly at odds with economic, political, and other realities: why did most oppressed African Americans embrace the dominant religion of their oppressors – in fact, the religion whose sacred text, the Bible, the Ku Klux Klan and other White segregationists used to justify the oppression of Blacks? And indeed, how did this very Christianity that was used (via a few cherry-picked and misconstrued verses from the Christian Bible) to justify human bondage and the brutal subjugation of the darker side of the Du Boisian world color line become not just a part of the African American experience in the nineteenth and twentieth centuries, but central and even essential to it?

Yet Black leaders – individuals such as Du Bois, Frederick Douglass, Betsy Stockton, Sojourner Truth, and (in Bonds's own time) Martin Luther King, Jr., among many others – transformed the world that was home to their oppressors, the world of their oppression, into (in Yolanda Pierce's terms, applied to literate Black writers of the antebellum period) a "New Jerusalem" – a place that offered a sense of home, community, solidarity, and – most of all – hope. They not only refuted the oppressors' narratives by demonstrating their own profoundly beautiful understanding of the Old and New Testaments alike and their oratorical genius, but also (and this where I believe the parallel to Margaret Bonds becomes most obvious) by telling new stories, by tendering narratives that, in Pierce's words, "challenged the idea that biblical rhetoric should be available for use only by those who supported slavery" and "proved that, indeed, the biblical word was a 'two-edged sword,' empowering the oppressed to vanquish the oppressor with language."[18]

In *The Montgomery Variations* Margaret Bonds told just such a new story. She used the rhetoric of White European orchestral music, variation sets, and program music that – for the overwhelming majority of the White orchestras and audiences who attended concerts of Bach and Richard Strauss – previously had been used to tell the stories of White male privilege while ignoring Whites' and males' disgraceful abuses of that privilege in an exclusionary culture that denied all but the most perfunctory recognition of African Americans, their stories, and their music. With these means, she told a new story all her own. That story was not an abstract philosophical mediation, a story of a sixteenth-century Spanish nobleman, or a glorification of the transfigurative demise of a person with whom those predominantly White and predominantly male performers and audiences could readily identify. It was, rather, the story of contemporary African Americans bravely fighting *against* the system that those performers and audiences, in the starkly segregated world of orchestral music in the mid-1960s, identified with by means of their race, their sex, and their privileged perspective. By virtue of the empathy that musical experience generates, in *The Montgomery Variations* the symbolic spiritual "I Want Jesus to Walk with Me" is no longer the music of those White male performers' and audiences' inimical Other, as it would normally be for privileged Whites in a world where integration was still a controversial term. Rather, in the context of Bonds's large-scale orchestral variations it is music that is *their own* as well as the music of the "benign God" who spreads love among all His children – "the good and the bad alike" – in that work's "Benediction" (No. 7). The *Credo* is even bolder in this regard, for in it Bonds sets to music overwhelmingly rooted in the White-dominated concert-music tradition the words of one of the African American world's most brilliant, prophetic, and revered authors – words that syncretize the most starkly antagonistic aspects of Black and White experience through their proclamation that the God of oppressed and oppressor made of "one blood" all people, even as those words resolutely affirm the beauty, dignity, and humanity of those whom the White-dominated world of orchestral–choral composition systemically, resolutely, and brutally subjugated.

One thing is certain: Margaret Bonds undertook the expressive challenge of creating these two works out of the deep and murky waters of unreconciled, and seemingly irreconcilable, musical and societal contradictions and conflicts out of a sense of responsibility, of doing what she had to in order to help right a great wrong. That sense of mission on behalf of the betterment of humanity through affirmation of Black art is evident in her declaration to Langston Hughes during one of his 1962 African mission trips that she was "delighted with [his] mission, and [knew] that this is what God want[ed] of [him]," and that she hoped that "in time our composers [in the US] [would] realize the importance of setting the poems of men of color."[19] It was also manifest in her efforts to get all NANM members to commit to purchasing music by Black composers every year, in her "Musico Negro" composer's group,[20] and in countless other activities. Her 1963 critical comparison of Adele Addison and Betty Allen clearly enunciates her conviction that artists of color were obligated to promote Black art, and her belief that failure to do so would affirm the segregated existence that had made the veil necessary to begin with even as it denied the world the benefits of the expressive art of those who lived within that veil.

Moreover, while Margaret Bonds's decision to affirm the inherent beauty, dignity, and humanity of the Black condition and Black experience, and to proclaim the divine mandate for racial justice and global equality in *The Montgomery Variations* and *Credo*, was ambitious, given their profoundly segregated musical and general social context, it was not a naïve miscalculation. She had lived within the Du Boisian veil all her life and had spent her entire career as an African American woman moving with extraordinary fluidity between the generally segregated musical domains of art song and popular song, between Black vernacular music and (stereotypically White) concert music that drank deeply of traditional European and White American classical traditions.

If one views *The Montgomery Variations* and the *Credo* in this context, then the aesthetic project of the *Variations* may be described as an elaborate instrumental counterpart to the tradition of concert spirituals. In this sense that work is an artistic gambit that originates from within the Du Boisian veil and uses the spiritual's emotive power to refute the artificial dichotomy of Black and White musical identities, and to generate empathy among Whites and Blacks alike for the plight of the courageous African Americans who were the victims of entrenched systemic racism and an oppressive caste system that denied their very humanity.[21] At the same time, the prominence of White European concert music, via J. S. Bach and Richard Strauss, within the *Variations* only raises the stakes in that artistic gambit, declaring the two traditionally segregated spheres as coequal and asserting that their desegregation would make possible an artistic and societal message that would remain unutterable as long as they were kept apart.

Having completed this gambit in *The Montgomery Variations*, however, Bonds then moved on to an even bolder one with the *Credo* – for even though that work does not employ a spiritual, it is the Black vernacular idiom of the gospel song, in "Especially Do I Believe in the Negro Race," that launches the curve of the arc toward racial justice in it. And that, together with Du Bois's powerful text itself, indelibly stamps the African American condition upon the music. Here the boldness of Bonds's compositional and societal gambit is augmented partly by the eloquence of the work's text and Du Bois's stature as towering figure in the quest for racial justice and global equality, but also by its inherent venture into the millennium-long and tradition-laden aesthetic territory of creeds and manifestos themselves. And the scale and scope of these two compositions combines with the inseparability of their elements that emanate from within the veil and without it to render them Margaret Bonds's personal rebuke of the non-sense and "devilish" nature of segregation and hatred, exploitation and oppression.

But the boldest artistic gambit in *The Montgomery Variations* and the *Credo* is this: that both works drink deeply of the Black sermonic tradition and offer redemption, peace, and hope to "black and brown and white" folk, to (in Bonds's words) "all [God's] children," oppressed and oppressors – "the good and the bad alike." In these works, racists, segregationists, and colonialist oppressors found words and music that showed them what Bonds considered God's true way, just as His oppressed found eloquent and beautiful reassurance that God was on their own side and they would ultimately prevail. With this gambit Bonds did not just confront a profoundly riven society and musical world, nor did she address herself to only one side of those warring forces. Rather, she confronted the very forces that generated the strife that threatened to tear that world asunder. *The Montgomery Variations* and *Credo* are, in this sense, musical and societal syncretisms and musical social-justice manifestos the likes of which the world had never seen before, and has never seen since.

Epilogue

A New [Musical] Jerusalem

Margaret Bonds wrote the following to Langston Hughes on December 11, 1961:

> I used to think of your poetry as "Langston's," but yesterday [when reading through your *Selected Poems*] I knew they don't belong to you at all. You gave them all to us.
> So it is with music. I write it and give it away to whosoever will carry or listen to the message.
> Carry this little light with you in your travels.[22]

"I write it and give it away to whosoever will carry or listen to the message": during early work on this book in the autumn of 2021, it was obvious that the "message" of Margaret Bonds's *Montgomery Variations* and *Credo* is even more needed now than it was when she wrote those works, and at that remains so today. (It is February 2023, just weeks after the murder of an unarmed Black man, twenty-nine-year-old Tyre Nichols (1993–2023), by five uniformed police officers trained to act in the knowledge that Black civilian life can be taken with impunity and without remorse. By the time this book comes off the press, many more instances of police brutality against Black folk will have been committed, most or perhaps all of them with the same immunity.) The quest for global equality is still beset from every side; the systemic racism and caste systems that threaten hopes of global freedom and brutally assault liberty especially for people of color are flourishing; and especially in the United States the tide of police-sanctioned violence against Black folk continues unabated. Ours is a world that desperately needs the "little light" that Margaret Bonds offered in her *Montgomery Variations* and *Credo*. If our time can embrace the light cast by those two manifestos, then perhaps we can appreciate them for what they are. Perhaps that appreciation will enrich our musical understanding of the progress that was made because of Du Bois's and Bonds's own vision. Most importantly, perhaps that understanding will enable our time, eventually, to achieve racial justice, gender justice, and global equality.

May we, all of us, heed the message of *The Montgomery Variations* and *Credo*, and carry it with us in our travels.

Notes

1. W. E. B. Du Bois, *The Souls of Black Folk: Essays and Sketches*, 3rd ed. (Chicago: A. C. McClurg, 1903), 3.

2. Margaret Bonds, speech for the Los Angeles Inner City Cultural Center's commemoration fo Langston Hughes's birthday, 1971 (Georgetown University Bonds Papers shelfmark GTM 130530 Box 5, folder 12).

3. See Margaret Bonds, "A Reminiscence," in *The Negro in Music and Art*, ed. Lindsay Patterson (New York: International Library of Negro Life and History, 1967), 190–93 at 192–93.

4. Bonds, "A Reminiscence," 192.

5. Reiland Rabaka, *Against Epistemic Apartheid: W. E. B. Du Bois and the Disciplinary Decadence of Sociology* (London: Lexington Books, 2010), 197.

6. See Chapter 1, pp. 21–24.

7. Christina Demaitre, "She Has a Musical Mission: Developing Racial Harmony; Heritage Motivates Composing Career," *The Washington Post* 87, no. 253 (August 14, 1964): C2.

8. See John Michael Cooper, "People of Color Who Write Classical Music: Recovering 'Lost' Music by Black Composers as Resistance and Revolution," *Black History Bulletin* 82, no. 1 (Spring 2019): 20–27.

9. See especially Eileen Southern, *The Music of Black Americans: A History*, 3rd ed. (New York: W. W. Norton, 1997), 311–12, 579–94.

10. See Doris Evans McGinty, "'As Large as She Can Make It': The Role of Black Women Activists in Music, 1880–1945," in *Cultivating Music in America: Women Patrons and Activists Since 1860*, ed. Ralph P. Locke and Cyrilla Barr (Berkeley: University of California Press, 1997), 214–36; further, Samantha Ege, "Composing a Symphonist: Florence Price and the Hand of Black Women's Fellowship," *Women in Music: A Journal of Gender and Culture* 24 (2020): 7–27.

11. Campbell Gibson, Kay Jung, and United States Bureau of the Census, *Historical Census Statistics on Population Totals by Race, 1790 to 1990, and by Hispanic Origin, 1970 to 1990, for the United States, Regions, Divisions, and States*, Population Division Working Paper Series, No. 56. (Washington, DC: U.S. Census Bureau, 2002), 98, 92, https://purl.fdlp.gov/GPO/LPS33172 (accessed June 26, 2021).

12. This is of course an extremely crude computation, failing as it does to account for significant variables such as region, budget, and other such variables.

13. Raymond Ericson, "The Fight for the Integrated Orchestra," *New York Times* (October 20, 1974), 174. The reported survey was conducted by the Symphony of the New World with assistance from the National Urban League.

14. See Brown, *The Heart of a Woman*, 158–60.
15. National Commission on the Observance of International Women's Year, *Suggested Guidelines for a Workshop on Improving the Status of Women in the Arts and Humanities* Appendix CC, 6.
16. See Jeffrey S. Sposato, *The Price of Assimilation: Felix Mendelssohn and the Nineteenth-Century Anti-Semitic Tradition* (Oxford: Oxford University Press, 2006), esp. 177–80.
17. The Northwestern University *Bulletin* shows that during Margaret Bonds's time there the textbook used in the music history courses she was required to take was Waldo Selden Pratt, *The History of Music: A Handbook and Guide for Students* (New York: G. Schirmer, 1907). This text does not mention Wagner's anti-Semitism, but it does draw attention to Mendelssohn's Jewish heritage as well as his Christian faith (pp. 516–21).
18. Yolanda Pierce, *Hell without Fires: Slavery, Christianity, and the Antebellum Scriptural Narrative* (Gainesville: University Press of Florida, 2005), 133.
19. Bonds (New York) to Hughes (New York), July 14, 1962 (Yale JWJ 26, Box 16, folder 378: no. 343).
20. Bonds (New York) to Hughes (New York), December 27, 1955 (Yale JWJ MSS 26, Box 16, folder 372).
21. See Sandra Jean Graham, *Spirituals and the Birth of a Black Entertainment Industry* (Urbana: University of Illinois Press, 2018), 249–50.
22. Bonds (New York) to Hughes (n.p.), December 11, 1961 (Yale JWJ 26, Box 16, folder 376: 315).

INDEX

Index

Index

Index

Printed in the United States
by Baker & Taylor Publisher Services